# Your All-in-One Resource

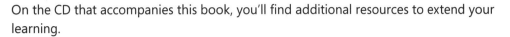 P9-CRS-684

On the CD that accompanies this book, you'll find additional resources to extend your learning.

The reference library includes the following fully searchable titles:

- *Microsoft Computer Dictionary*, 5th ed.
- *First Look 2007 Microsoft Office System* by Katherine Murray
- Windows Vista Product Guide

Also provided are a sample chapter and poster from *Look Both Ways: Help Protect Your Family on the Internet* by Linda Criddle.

The CD interface has a new look. You can use the tabs for an assortment of tasks:

- Check for book updates (if you have Internet access)
- Install the book's practice file
- Go online for product support or CD support
- Send us feedback

The following screen shot gives you a glimpse of the new interface.

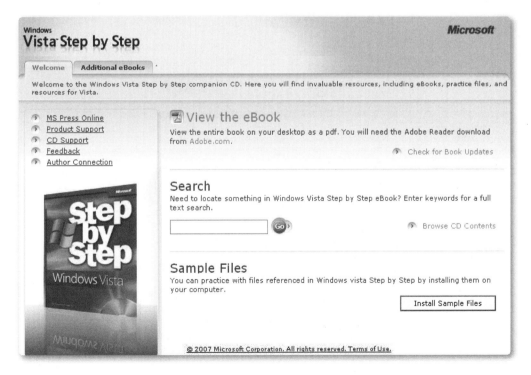

# Microsoft® Office
# Publisher 2007
# Step by Step

*Joyce Cox and Joan Preppernau*
*Online Training Solutions, Inc.*

Comsewogue Public Library
170 Terryville Road
Port Jefferson Station, NY 11776

PUBLISHED BY
Microsoft Press
A Division of Microsoft Corporation
One Microsoft Way
Redmond, Washington 98052-6399

Copyright © 2008 by Online Training Solutions, Inc.

All rights reserved. No part of the contents of this book may be reproduced or transmitted in any form or by any means without the written permission of the publisher.

Library of Congress Control Number: 2007930349

Printed and bound in the United States of America.

3 4 5 6 7 8 9   QWT   2 1 0 9 8

Distributed in Canada by H.B. Fenn and Company Ltd.

A CIP catalogue record for this book is available from the British Library.

Microsoft Press books are available through booksellers and distributors worldwide. For further information about international editions, contact your local Microsoft Corporation office or contact Microsoft Press International directly at fax (425) 936-7329. Visit our Web site at www.microsoft.com/mspress. Send comments to mspinput@microsoft.com.

Microsoft, Microsoft Press, Aero, Excel, Expression, FrontPage, Groove, Hotmail, InfoPath, Internet Explorer, OneNote, Outlook, PowerPoint, SharePoint, Visio, Windows, Windows Server, and Windows Vista are either registered trademarks or trademarks of Microsoft Corporation in the United States and/or other countries. Other product and company names mentioned herein may be the trademarks of their respective owners.

The example companies, organizations, products, domain names, e-mail addresses, logos, people, places, and events depicted herein are fictitious. No association with any real company, organization, product, domain name, e-mail address, logo, person, place, or event is intended or should be inferred.

This book expresses the author's views and opinions. The information contained in this book is provided without any express, statutory, or implied warranties. Neither the authors, Microsoft Corporation, nor its resellers, or distributors will be held liable for any damages caused or alleged to be caused either directly or indirectly by this book.

**Acquisitions Editor:** Juliana Aldous Atkins
**Developmental Editor:** Sandra Haynes
**Project Editor:** Rosemary Caperton
**Editorial Production Services:** Online Training Solutions, Inc.

Body Part No. X13-86333

# Contents

**What do you think of this book? We want to hear from you!**

Microsoft is interested in hearing your feedback so we can continually improve our books and learning resources for you. To participate in a brief online survey, please visit:

**www.microsoft.com/learning/booksurvey/**

**What do you think of this book? We want to hear from you!**

Microsoft is interested in hearing your feedback so we can continually improve our books and learning resources for you. To participate in a brief online survey, please visit:

**www.microsoft.com/learning/booksurvey/**

# About the Authors

## Joyce Cox

Joyce has 25 years' experience in the development of training materials about technical subjects for non-technical audiences, and is the author of dozens of books about Microsoft Office and Windows technologies. She is the Vice President of Online Training Solutions, Inc. (OTSI). She was President of and principal author for Online Press, where she developed the *Quick Course* series of computer training books for beginning and intermediate adult learners. She was also the first managing editor of Microsoft Press, an editor for Sybex, and an editor for the University of California.

Joyce and her husband Ted live in downtown Bellevue, Washington, and escape as often as they can to their tiny, offline cabin in the Cascade foothills.

## Joan Preppernau

Joan has worked in the training and certification industry for 10 years. As President of OTSI, Joan is responsible for guiding the translation of technical information and requirements into useful, relevant, and measurable training, learning, and certification deliverables. Joan is the author of more than a dozen books about Windows and Office applications, and a contributor to the development of certification exams for the 2007 Office system applications and Windows Vista.

Joan has lived and worked in New Zealand, Sweden, Denmark, and various locations in the U.S. during the past 16 years. Having finally discovered the delights of a daily dose of sunshine, Joan is now happily ensconced in America's Finest City—San Diego, California—with her husband Barry and their daughter Trinity.

# The Team

Without the support of the hard-working members of the OTSI publishing team, this book would not exist. Barry Preppernau provided technical review services. Robert (RJ) Cadranell guided the production process. Lisa Van Every laid out the book using Adobe InDesign, and Jaime Odell provided quality control and editorial support. Susie Bayers, Marlene Lambert, and Jean Trenary tied up loose ends and, as always, did whatever was necessary to create an excellent product. Nancy Guenther created the index, and Rosemary Caperton provided invaluable support on behalf of Microsoft Press.

# Online Training Solutions, Inc. (OTSI)

OTSI specializes in the design, creation, and production of Office and Windows training products for information workers and home computer users. For more information about OTSI, visit

*www.otsi.com*

# Introducing Publisher 2007

Microsoft Office Publisher 2007 is a desktop publishing program with which you can create a wide variety of professional-looking publications intended for print or online presentation. Publisher provides well-thought-out templates to help you structure content within a publication (or you can start from scratch), and professionally designed color palettes that can quickly change an amateur publication into a masterpiece.

When designing multiple publications for an organization, you can automatically incorporate brand elements such as colors, fonts, and logos into business stationery, brochures, newsletters, cards, catalogs, and many other publications. After you create a publication, Publisher helps you to print it, package it for professional printing, distribute it by e-mail, or publish it to a Web site.

## New Features

Publisher 2007 has a lot of neat new features that simplify the process of creating a classy publication. We don't indicate which features are new within the book, but we do list them here. To locate information about a specific feature, see the index at the back of this book.

If you're upgrading to Publisher 2007 from a previous version, you're probably more interested in the differences between the old and new versions and how they will affect you than you are in the basic functionality of Publisher. To help you identify the entire scope of change from the version of Publisher you're familiar with, we've listed here the new features introduced in Publisher 2007 and in Publisher 2003.

### If You Are Upgrading from Publisher 2003

Use these new features to create high-quality branded publications and marketing collateral:

- **Apply your brand in one step**  With Publisher 2007, you can easily apply and view elements from your brand—logo, colors, fonts, and business information—to all templates, in one step.

- **Template search**  Quickly find just the right template within Publisher 2007 or on Microsoft Office Online. Preview Office Online templates within Publisher 2007.

- **Office Online templates preview**  When connected to the Internet, you can access hundreds of Publisher templates available on Office Online right from within Publisher 2007.

- **Publisher Tasks**  Use new Publisher Tasks in Publisher 2007 for help with common Publisher creation and distribution procedures.

- **Store frequently used design elements**  Store and reuse text, graphics, and design elements across Publisher publications by using the Content Library.

Use these new features to create effective online marketing campaigns:

- **Personalized e-mail with E-Mail Merge**  Create and send personalized marketing communications by e-mail using E-mail Merge.

- **Personalized hyperlinks**  Personalize the display text and hyperlinks to further personalize your e-mail merge communications.

- **Improve navigation with bookmarks**  Add bookmarks to help readers quickly browse publications and e-mail messages.

- **Apply an e-mail template to publications**  Convert a multiple-page publication such as a newsletter, add bookmarks, and distribute it as an e-mail message.

- **Check your e-mail design**  Identify and correct potential problems with e-mail publications, such as text converted to an image, with the enhanced Design Checker.

Use these new features to manage and personalize lists:

- **Combine lists within Publisher**  Combine, edit, and save lists from multiple sources—including Microsoft Office Excel 2007, Microsoft Office Outlook 2007, and Microsoft Office Access 2007—within Publisher 2007 to create personalized print and e-mail materials or to build a publication by using Catalog Merge.

- **Personalized hyperlinks**  Personalize the display text and hyperlinks to further personalize your e-mail merge communications.

- **Personalization tips with Publisher Tasks**  Use Publisher Tasks to learn how to prepare a mailing list, and get tips for personalizing a mailing list, purchasing a mailing list, and using mailing services.

Use these new features to share, print, and publish publications:

- **Publish in PDF or XPS format**  After installing a free add-in, you can save Publisher files in PDF or XPS file format for sharing, online viewing, and printing.

- **Create press-ready PDF files**  For commercial printers using a PDF workflow, press-ready PDF files from Publisher 2007 means easier acceptance of Publisher files.

Use these new features to integrate Publisher with Microsoft Office Outlook 2007 with Business Contact Manager:

- **Create a new marketing campaign** Initiate a new marketing campaign using Outlook 2007 with Business Contact Manager from a new toolbar within Publisher. Identify lists of Business Contacts or Accounts to which to distribute publications.

- **Link to Business Contacts for tracking** Create a flyer, newsletter, e-mail message, or other publication, and indicate which Business Contacts, Accounts, Opportunities, or Business Projects within Outlook 2007 with Business Contact Manager are to receive your publication.

- **Search folders** With improved Mail Merge and E-mail Merge functionality, you can now choose Outlook contacts saved to Search Folders.

## If You Are Upgrading from Publisher 2002

In addition to the features listed in the previous section, if you're upgrading from Publisher 2002 (part of the Microsoft Office XP program suite), you'll find the following:

- **Catalog Merge** Use Catalog Merge to build custom materials, such as datasheets or catalogs, by merging text and images from a database—for example, those in Access, Excel, or Outlook.

- **Baseline alignment and guides** Improve the appearance of text by aligning text across multiple columns and evenly spacing text in columns. You can also align text to a baseline guide.

- **Start your own template library** Easily save, categorize, and access your own branded templates in My Templates within Publisher 2007.

- **Save as picture** Group and save design elements as graphics, and specify the image format and resolution you want to use in other programs.

- **E-mail templates** Choose from dozens of e-mail publication templates for a quick start to your e-mail communications.

- **Incremental Web site upload** Upload only the changes to a publication that has already been posted to a Web server.

- **CMYK composite postscript** Create process-color (CMYK) composite postscript files, a feature highly requested by commercial printers that makes it easier for you to get your Publisher publications commercially printed.

- **Advanced print settings** Create separations directly from the Print dialog box, including converting spot colors to process colors.

# Publisher Basics

As with all programs in the 2007 Microsoft Office release, the most common way to start Publisher is from the Start menu displayed when you click the Start button at the left end of the Windows taskbar.

When you are working in a publication, here are a few things to know about the contents of the Publisher program window:

- The *title bar* displays the name of the active document. At the right end of the title bar are the three familiar buttons that have the same function in all Windows programs. You can temporarily hide the Publisher window by clicking the Minimize button, adjust the size of the window with the Restore Down/Maximize button, and close the active document or quit Word with the Close button.

- Some button names are displayed and some aren't. Pausing the mouse pointer over any button for a few seconds (called *hovering*) displays a *ScreenTip* with not only the button's name but also its function.

- Some buttons have arrows, but not all arrows are alike. If you point to a button and both the button and its arrow are in the same box and are the same color, clicking the button will display options for refining the action of the button. If you point to a button and the button is in one box and its arrow is in a different box with a different shade, clicking the button will carry out that action with the button's current settings. If you want to change those settings, you need to click the arrow to see the available options.

- Across the bottom of the program window, the *status bar* gives you information about the current document.

# Let's Get Started!

Publisher is a fun program to use, and after becoming familiar with the basic tools and techniques, there is practically no limit to the types of publications you can create. This book gives you straightforward instructions for using Publisher. It takes you from knowing little or nothing about Publisher—or, for that matter, about desktop publishing—to a level of expertise that will enable you to create professional-looking publications for printing or Web distribution. We look forward to showing you around Microsoft Office Publisher 2007.

# Information for Readers Running Windows XP

The graphics and the operating system–related instructions in this book reflect the Windows Vista user interface. However, Windows Vista is not required; you can also use a computer running Windows XP.

Most of the differences you will encounter when working through the exercises in this book on a Windows XP computer center around appearance rather than functionality. For example, the Windows Vista Start button is round rather than rectangular and is not labeled with the word *Start*; window frames and window-management buttons look different; and if your system supports Windows Aero, the window frames might be transparent.

In this section, we provide steps for navigating to or through menus and dialog boxes in Windows XP that differ from those provided in the exercises in this book. For the most part, these differences are small enough that you will have no difficulty in completing the exercises.

## Managing the Practice Files

The instructions given in the "Using the Book's CD" section are specific to Windows Vista. The only differences when installing, using, uninstalling, and removing the practice files supplied on the companion CD are the default installation location and the uninstall process.

On a Windows Vista computer, the default installation location of the practice files is *Documents\Microsoft Press\SBS_Publisher2007*. On a Windows XP computer, the default installation location is *My Documents\Microsoft Press\SBS_Publisher2007*. If your computer is running Windows XP, whenever an exercise tells you to navigate to your *Documents* folder, you should instead go to your *My Documents* folder.

To uninstall the practice files from a Windows XP computer:

1. On the Windows taskbar, click the **Start** button, and then click **Control Panel**.
2. In **Control Panel**, click (or in Classic view, double-click) **Add or Remove Programs**.

3. In the **Add or Remove Programs** window, click **Microsoft Office Publisher 2007 Step by Step**, and then click **Remove**.

4. In the **Add or Remove Programs** message box asking you to confirm the deletion, click **Yes**.

> **Important** If you need help installing or uninstalling the practice files, please see the "Getting Help" section later in this book. Microsoft Product Support Services does not provide support for this book or its companion CD.

# Using the Start Menu

To start Microsoft Office Publisher 2007 on a Windows XP computer:

→ Click the **Start** button, point to **All Programs**, click **Microsoft Office**, and then click **Microsoft Office Publisher 2007**.

Folders on the Windows Vista Start menu expand vertically. Folders on the Windows XP Start menu expand horizontally. However, the steps to access a command on the Start menu are identical on both systems.

# Navigating Dialog Boxes

On a Windows XP computer, some of the dialog boxes you will work with in the exercises not only look different from the graphics shown in this book but also work differently. These dialog boxes are primarily those that act as an interface between Publisher and the operating system, including any dialog box in which you navigate to a specific location.

For example, to navigate to the *GettingStarted* folder in Windows XP:

→ On the **Places** bar, click **My Documents**. Then in the folder content pane, double-click **Microsoft Press**, **SBS_Publisher2007**, and then **GettingStarted**.

To move back to the *SBS_Publisher2007* folder in Windows XP:

Up One Level

→ On the toolbar, click the **Up One Level** button.

# Features and Conventions of This Book

This book has been designed to lead you step by step through all the tasks you are most likely to want to perform in Microsoft Office Publisher 2007. If you start at the beginning and work your way through all the exercises, you will gain enough proficiency to be able to create quite elaborate publications with Publisher. However, each topic is self contained. If you have worked with a previous version of Publisher, or if you completed all the exercises and later need help remembering how to perform a procedure, the following features of this book will help you locate specific information:

- **Detailed table of contents.** A listing of the topics and sidebars within each chapter.
- **Chapter thumb tabs.** Easily locate the beginning of the chapter you want.
- **Topic-specific running heads.** Within a chapter, quickly locate the topic you want by looking at the running head of odd-numbered pages.
- **Quick Reference.** General instructions for each procedure covered in specific detail elsewhere in the book. Refresh your memory about a task while working with your own documents.
- **Detailed index.** Look up specific tasks and features and general concepts in the index, which has been carefully crafted with the reader in mind.
- **Companion CD.** Contains the practice files needed for the step-by-step exercises, as well as a fully searchable electronic version of this book and other useful resources.

In addition, we provide a glossary of terms for those times when you need to look up the meaning of a word or the definition of a concept.

You can save time when you use this book by understanding how the *Step by Step* series shows special instructions, keys to press, buttons to click, and so on.

| Convention | Meaning |
|---|---|
| | This icon at the end of a chapter introduction indicates information about the practice files provided on the companion CD for use in the chapter. |
| USE | This paragraph preceding a step-by-step exercise indicates the practice files that you will use when working through the exercise. |
| BE SURE TO | This paragraph preceding or following an exercise indicates any requirements you should attend to before beginning the exercise or actions you should take to restore your system after completing the exercise. |
| OPEN | This paragraph preceding a step-by-step exercise indicates files that you should open before beginning the exercise. |
| CLOSE | This paragraph following a step-by-step exercise provides instructions for closing open files or programs before moving on to another topic. |
| 1<br>2 | Blue numbered steps guide you through step-by-step exercises and Quick Reference versions of procedures. |
| 1<br>2 | Black numbered steps guide you through procedures in sidebars and expository text. |
| → | An arrow indicates a procedure that has only one step. |
| **See Also** | These paragraphs direct you to more information about a given topic in this book or elsewhere. |
| Troubleshooting | These paragraphs explain how to fix a common problem that might prevent you from continuing with an exercise. |
| Tip | These paragraphs provide a helpful hint or shortcut that makes working through a task easier, or information about other available options. |
| Important | These paragraphs point out information that you need to know to complete a procedure. |
| Ctrl + Home | A plus sign (+) between two key names means that you must hold down the first key while you press the second key. For example, "press Ctrl + Home" means "hold down the Ctrl key while you press the Home key." |
| **Program interface elements** | In steps, the names of program elements, such as buttons, commands, and dialog boxes, are shown in black bold characters. |
| User input | Anything you are supposed to type appears in blue bold characters. |
| *Glossary terms* | Terms that are explained in the glossary at the end of the book are shown in blue italic characters. |

# Using the Book's CD

The companion CD included with this book contains the practice files you'll use as you work through the book's exercises, as well as other electronic resources that will help you learn how to use Microsoft Office Publisher 2007.

## What's on the CD?

The following table lists the practice files supplied on the book's CD.

| Chapter | Files |
| --- | --- |
| Chapter 1:<br>Getting Started with Publisher 2007 | Importing.docx<br>Logo.png<br>Opening.pub<br>Printing.pub |
| Chapter 2:<br>Creating Visual Interest | Birthday at the Ritz.png<br>Text.docx |
| Chapter 3:<br>Creating Colorful Cards and Calendars | Arizona10.jpg<br>DataSource.xlsx<br>FoldedCard.pub<br>Postcard.pub |
| Chapter 4:<br>Marketing Your Product, Service,<br>or Organization | Brochure.pub<br>BusinessCard.pub<br>Envelope.pub<br>Flyer.pub<br>Icon.png<br>Invoice.pub<br>Name.png |
| Chapter 5:<br>Creating Text-Based Publications | ADatumNews.pub |
| Chapter 6:<br>Communicating Your Message Online | BookSeries.pub<br>WineTasting.pub |

In addition to the practice files, the CD contains some exciting resources that will really enhance your ability to get the most out of using this book and Publisher 2007, including the following eBooks:

- *Microsoft Office Publisher 2007 Step by Step*
- *Microsoft Computer Dictionary*, 5th ed.
- *First Look 2007 Microsoft Office System* (Katherine Murray, 2006)
- Sample chapter and poster from *Look Both Ways: Help Protect Your Family on the Internet* (Linda Criddle, 2007)
- Microsoft Office Fluent Ribbon Quick Reference
- Windows Vista Product Guide

> **Important** The companion CD for this book does not contain the Publisher 2007 software. You should purchase and install that program before using this book.

# Minimum System Requirements

## 2007 Microsoft Office System

The 2007 Microsoft Office system includes the following programs:

- Microsoft Office Access 2007
- Microsoft Office Communicator 2007
- Microsoft Office Excel 2007
- Microsoft Office Groove 2007
- Microsoft Office InfoPath 2007
- Microsoft Office OneNote 2007
- Microsoft Office Outlook 2007
- Microsoft Office Outlook 2007 with Business Contact Manager
- Microsoft Office PowerPoint 2007
- Microsoft Office Publisher 2007
- Microsoft Office Word 2007

No single edition of the 2007 Microsoft Office system installs all of the above programs. Specialty programs available separately include Microsoft Office Project 2007, Microsoft Office SharePoint Designer 2007, and Microsoft Office Visio 2007.

To run these programs, your computer needs to meet the following minimum requirements:

- 500 megahertz (MHz) processor
- 256 megabytes (MB) RAM
- CD or DVD drive
- 2 gigabyte (GB) hard disk space for installation; a portion of this disk space will be freed if you select the option to delete the installation files

> **Tip** Hard disk requirements will vary depending on configuration; custom installation choices may require more or less hard disk space.

- Monitor with 800 × 600 screen resolution; 1024 × 768 or higher recommended
- Keyboard and mouse or compatible pointing device
- Internet connection, 128 kilobits per second (Kbps) or greater, for download and activation of products, accessing Microsoft Office Online and online Help topics, and any other Internet-dependent processes
- Windows Vista or later, Microsoft Windows XP with Service Pack 2 (SP2), or Microsoft Windows Server 2003 or later
- Windows Internet Explorer 7 or Microsoft Internet Explorer 6 with service packs

The 2007 Microsoft Office suites, including Office Basic 2007, Office Home & Student 2007, Office Standard 2007, Office Small Business 2007, Office Professional 2007, Office Ultimate 2007, Office Professional Plus 2007, and Office Enterprise 2007, all have similar requirements.

## Step-by-Step Exercises

In addition to the hardware, software, and connections required to run the 2007 Microsoft Office system, you will need the following to successfully complete the exercises in this book:

- Publisher 2007, Word 2007, and Outlook 2007
- Access to a printer
- 4 MB of available hard disk space for the practice files

# Installing the Practice Files

You need to install the practice files to a suitable location on your hard disk before you can use them in the exercises. Follow these steps:

1. Remove the companion CD from the envelope at the back of the book, and insert it into the CD drive of your computer.

   The Step By Step Companion CD License Terms appear. Follow the on-screen directions. To use the practice files, you must accept the terms of the license agreement. After you accept the license agreement, a menu screen appears.

   > **Important** If the menu screen does not appear, click the Start button and then click Computer. Display the Folders list in the Navigation Pane, click the icon for your CD drive, and then in the right pane, double-click the StartCD executable file.

2. Click **Install Practice Files**.

3. Click **Next** on the first screen, and then click **Next** to accept the terms of the license agreement on the next screen.

4. If you want to install the practice files to a location other than the default folder (*Documents\Microsoft Press\SBS_Publisher2007*), click the **Change** button, select the new drive and path, and then click **OK**.

   > **Important** If you install the practice files to a location other than the default, you will need to substitute that path within the exercises.

5. Click **Next** on the **Choose Destination Location** screen, and then click **Install** on the **Ready to Install the Program** screen to install the selected practice files.

6. After the practice files have been installed, click **Finish**.

7. Close the **Step by Step Companion CD** window, remove the companion CD from the CD drive, and return it to the envelope at the back of the book.

# Using the Practice Files

When you install the practice files from the companion CD that accompanies this book, the files are stored on your hard disk in *Documents\Microsoft Press\SBS_Publisher2007*. Each exercise is preceded by a paragraph that lists the files needed for that exercise and explains any preparations needed before you start working through the exercise. Here are examples:

> **USE** the *Opening* publication. This practice file is located in the *Documents\Microsoft Press\ SBS_Publisher2007\GettingStarted* folder.
>
> **BE SURE TO** start your computer, but don't start Publisher before starting this exercise.

You can browse to the practice files in Windows Explorer by following these steps:

Start

1. On the Windows taskbar, click the **Start** button, and then click **Documents**.

2. In your **Documents** folder, double-click **MSP**, double-click **SBS_Publisher2007**, and then double-click a specific chapter folder.

You can browse to the practice files from a Publisher 2007 Open Publication dialog box by following these steps:

1. In the **Favorite Links** pane in the dialog box, click **Documents**.

2. In your **Documents** folder, double-click **Microsoft Press**, double-click **SBS_Publisher2007**, and then double-click the specified chapter folder.

# Removing and Uninstalling the Practice Files

After you finish working through this book, delete the practice documents, messages, and other items you created while working through the exercises, and then uninstall the practice files that were installed from the companion CD. Follow these steps:

Start

1. On the Windows taskbar, click the **Start** button, and then click **Control Panel**.

2. In **Control Panel**, under **Programs**, click the **Uninstall a program** task.

3. In the **Programs and Features** window, click **Microsoft Office Publisher 2007 Step by Step**, and then on the toolbar at the top of the window, click the **Uninstall** button.

4. If the **Programs and Features** message box asking you to confirm the deletion appears, click **Yes**.

**See Also** If you need additional help installing or uninstalling the practice files, see "Getting Help" later in this book.

> **Important** Microsoft Product Support Services does not provide support for this book or its companion CD.

# Getting Help

Every effort has been made to ensure the accuracy of this book and the contents of its companion CD. If you do run into problems, please contact the sources listed below for assistance.

## Getting Help with This Book and Its Companion CD

If your question or issue concerns the content of this book or its companion CD, please first search the online Microsoft Press Knowledge Base, which provides support information for known errors in or corrections to this book, at the following Web site:

*www.microsoft.com/mspress/support/search.asp*

If you do not find your answer in the online Knowledge Base, or if you experience a technical difficulty with the companion CD, send your comments or questions to Microsoft Press Technical Support at:

*mspinput@microsoft.com*

## Getting Help with Publisher 2007

If your question is about Microsoft Office Publisher 2007, and not about the content of this Microsoft Press book, your first recourse is the Publisher Help system. This system is a combination of tools and files stored on your computer when you installed the 2007 Microsoft Office system and, if your computer is connected to the Internet, information available from Microsoft Office Online. There are several ways to find general or specific Help information:

- To find out about an item on the screen, you can display a *ScreenTip*. For example, to display a ScreenTip for a button, point to the button without clicking it. The ScreenTip gives the button's name and the associated keyboard shortcut, if there is one.

- From the Publisher program window, you can display the Publisher Help window by clicking Microsoft Office Publisher Help on the Help menu.

- After opening a dialog box, you can click the Help button (also a question mark) at the right end of the dialog box title bar to display the Publisher Help window with topics related to the functions of that dialog box.

To practice getting help, you can work through the following exercise.

**BE SURE TO** start Publisher before beginning this exercise.

1. At the right end of the menu bar, click the **Type a question for help** box.

2. Type How do I get help? and then press Enter .

   The Publisher Help window opens.

3. Click the **Get help from Microsoft Support Services** topic.

   Read about getting product support from Microsoft.

4. Click the **Back** button

Back

5. Scroll down and click **Print a Help topic**.

   Read about printing a help topic so that you can save it for future reference.

Home

6. On the toolbar, click the **Home** button.

The main Publisher help window opens.

Show Table of
Contents

7. In the list of topics in the **Publisher Help** window, click **Activating Publisher**.

Publisher Help displays a list of topics related to activating Microsoft Office system programs. You can click any topic to display the corresponding information.

8. On the toolbar, click the **Show Table of Contents** button.

The Table Of Contents appears in the left pane, organized by category, like the table of contents in a book.

Clicking any category (represented by a book icon) displays that category's topics (represented by help icons).

Category

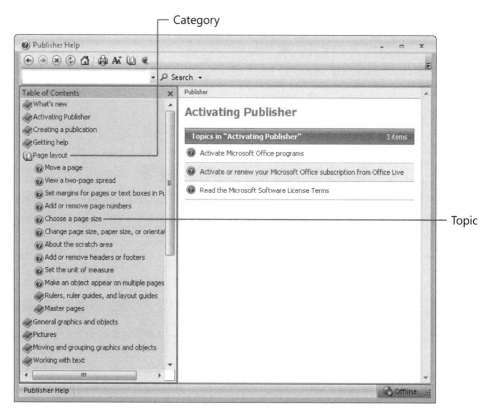

Topic

If you're connected to the Internet, Publisher displays categories, topics, and training available from the Office Online Web site as well as those stored on your computer.

Forward

9. In the **Table of Contents**, click a few categories and topics, then click the **Back** and **Forward** buttons to move among the topics you have already viewed.

**CLOSE** the Publisher Help window.

# More Information

If your question is about Microsoft Office Publisher 2007 or another Microsoft software product and you cannot find the answer in the product's Help system, please search the appropriate product solution center or the Microsoft Knowledge Base at:

*support.microsoft.com*

In the United States, Microsoft software product support issues not covered by the Microsoft Knowledge Base are addressed by Microsoft Product Support Services. Location-specific software support options are available from:

*support.microsoft.com/gp/selfoverview/*

# Quick Reference

## 1 Getting Started with Publisher 2007

**To start Publisher, page 4**

→ On the **Start** menu, click **All Programs**, click **Microsoft Office**, and then click **Microsoft Office Publisher 2007**.

**To display the Getting Started window, page 4**

→ Close any open publications, or click **New** on the **File** menu.

**To bypass the Getting Started window, page 4**

1. On the **Tools** menu, click **Options**.
2. On the **General** tab of the **Options** dialog box, clear the **Show Publication Types when starting Publisher** check box, and then click **OK**.

**To create a publication based on a ready-made Publisher template, page 4**

1. In the **Publication Types** list, click the publication category you want.
2. In the center pane, click the thumbnail of the design you want.
3. In the right pane, set the publication options. Then click **Create**.

**To change the template or type of an existing publication, page 7**

1. In the **Format Publication** task pane, under *Publication Type* **Options**, click **Change Template**.
2. In the **Change Template** window, click the new layout or publication you want to use.

**To import a Microsoft Office Word document, page 8**

1. In the **Publication Types** list, click **Import Word Documents**. In the center pane, click the design template you want to apply to the imported document.
2. In the right pane, under **Customize**, select the **Color scheme**, **Font scheme**, and **Business information**.

3. Under **Options**, select the **Page size** and **Columns**, and if you want to include a title page, select that check box. Then click **Create**.

4. In the **Import Word Document** dialog box, select the file you want to import, and then click **OK**.

**To save a publication in a new folder, page 13**

1. On the **File** menu, click **Save As**.

2. On the toolbar of the **Save As** dialog box, click the **New Folder** button.

3. Type a name for the folder, press <kbd>Enter</kbd>, name the file if necessary, and then click **Save**.

**To save a publication as a template, page 14**

1. On the **File** menu, click **Save As**.

2. In the **Save As** dialog box, enter a name for the template in the **File name** box.

3. Click the **Save as type** arrow, and then in the list, click **Publisher Template**.

4. If you want to assign the template to a specific category, click the **Change** button. Select the category from the list or select the current category and type the name of a new category. Then click **OK**.

5. Click **Save**.

**To create a new publication based on a custom template, page 14**

1. In the left pane of the Getting Started window, under **Microsoft Publisher**, click **My Templates**.

2. In the center pane, click the template you want. Then click **Create**.

**To open an existing publication, page 17**

1. In the **Recent Publications** pane of the Getting Started window, click **From File**.

2. In the **Open Publication** dialog box, browse to and select the file you want to open, and then click **Open**.

**To move from page to page within a publication, page 17**

→ On the page sorter at the bottom of the window, click the page you want to display.

**To change the zoom level of a publication, page 18**

→ On the **Standard** toolbar, click the **Zoom** arrow, and then select the **Zoom** level you want.

or

→ On the **Standard** toolbar, click the **Zoom In** or **Zoom Out** button.

**To create an information set, page 20**

→ In the **Publication Types** list, click any publication type. Then in the right pane, under **Customize**, in the **Business information** list, click **Create new**.

or

1. In an open publication, on the **Edit** menu, click **Business Information**.

2. In the **Create New Business Information Set** dialog box, enter information you want to save as part of the information set. If any information does not apply, delete it.

3. Below the **Logo** box, click **Remove** to clear the current logo, or click **Change** and then in the **Insert Picture** dialog box, browse to and select the logo you want to use, and click **Open**.

4. In the **Business Information set name** box, enter a name for the information set. Then click **Save**.

**To preview a publication as it will appear when printed, page 24**

→ On the **Standard** toolbar, click the **Print Preview** button.

**To print a publication, page 25**

1. On the **File** menu, click **Print**.

2. In the **Print** dialog box, change any settings that apply, and then click **OK**.

## 2 Creating Visual Interest

**To create a blank publication, page 32**

1. In the **Publication Types** list, click **Blank Page Sizes**. In the center pane, click the design you want.

2. In the right pane, under **Customize**, select the **Color scheme**, **Font scheme**, and **Business information**. Then click **Create**.

**To add a text box, page 33**

1. Click the **Text Box** button on the **Objects** toolbar, or click **Text Box** on the **Insert** menu.

2. Drag to draw a text box of the size you want.

**To insert the contents of an external document into a text box, page 34**

1. With the insertion point in the text box, click **Text File** on the **Insert** menu.
2. In the **Insert Text** dialog box, browse to and select the file you want, and click **OK**.

**To format a text box, page 34**

→ Double-click the text box frame. Then in the **Format Text Box** dialog box, make the formatting changes you want, and click **OK**.

**To format the text in a text box, page 35**

→ Select the text you want to format. Then use the commands on the **Format** menu or **Formatting** toolbar to make the changes you want.

**To add a WordArt object to a publication, page 39**

1. Click the **Insert WordArt** button on the **Objects** toolbar, or point to **Picture** on the **Insert** menu, and then click **WordArt**.
2. In the **WordArt Gallery**, click the style you want, and then click **OK**.
3. In the **Edit WordArt Text** dialog box, enter the text you want, and then click **OK**.

**To modify the appearance of a WordArt object, page 40**

1. Select the WordArt object. On the **WordArt** toolbar, click the **WordArt Shape** button, and then in the gallery, click the shape you want.
2. On the **WordArt** toolbar, click the **Format WordArt** button. In the **Format WordArt** dialog box, change any settings you want, and then click **OK**.

**To add an image from a file to the Clip Organizer, page 44**

1. At the bottom of the **Clip Art** task pane, click **Organize clips**.
2. In the **Collection List** pane of the Microsoft Clip Organizer window, under **My Collections**, click the **Favorites** folder.
3. On the window's **File** menu, point to **Add Clips to Organizer**, and then click **On My Own**.
4. In the **Add Clips to Organizer** dialog box, browse to and select the file you want to add, and then click **Add**.

**To delete a clip art image from the Clip Organizer, page 44**

→ In the **Microsoft Clip Organizer** window, point to the image, click the arrow that appears, click **Delete From Clip Organizer**, and then click **OK** to confirm the deletion.

**To add keywords to an image, page 44**

1. In the **Microsoft Clip Organizer** window, point to the image, click the arrow that appears, and then click **Edit Keywords**.

2. In the **Keyword** box of the **Keywords** dialog box, type the word or words that you want to associate with this file (separating words and phrases with commas), and then click **Add**.

**To insert a clip art image, page 46**

1. Click the **Picture Frame** button on the **Objects** toolbar or point to **Picture** on the **Insert** menu, and then click **Clip Art**.

2. In the **Clip Art** task pane, do the following:

   a. In the **Search for** box, enter a word or words describing the picture you want.

   b. In the **Search in** list, select the collections you want to search.

   c. In the **Results should be** list, select the file types you want the search to return.

   d. Click **Go**.

3. In the results list, click the thumbnail you want to insert.

4. Drag the image frame sizing handles to size the image to fit the available space.

**To insert an image from a file, page 49**

1. Click the **Picture Frame** button on the **Objects** toolbar, and then click **Picture from File**; or point to **Picture** on the **Insert** menu, and then click **From File**.

2. In the **Insert Picture** dialog box, browse to and select the picture you want to insert, and then click **Insert**.

**To display only a portion of an inserted image, page 50**

1. Select the image. Then on the **Picture** toolbar, click the **Crop** button.

2. Drag the cropping handles to position the crop marks where you want them.

**To delete the cropped area of an image or minimize the file size of an inserted image, page 51**

1. Select the image. Then on the **Picture** toolbar, click the **Compress Pictures** button.

2. In the **Compress Pictures** dialog box, set the compression options, target output, and scope. Then click **Compress**.

3. If Publisher prompts you to do so, click **Yes** to apply picture optimization.

**To insert a shape, page 54**

1. Click the **AutoShapes** button on the **Objects** toolbar or point to **Picture** on the **Insert** menu, and then click **AutoShapes**.

2. On the detachable **AutoShapes** toolbar, point to the shape category you want, and then click the shape you want to insert.

3. Drag the pointer across the page to draw a shape of the size you want.

**To format shapes, page 54**

1. To change the shape's direction, on the **Arrange** menu, point to **Rotate or Flip**, and then click **Flip Vertical**.

2. Double-click the shape, and on the **Colors and Lines** tab of the **Format AutoShape** dialog box, change the **Color** setting under **Fill** to what you want, and change any other settings you want. Then select the **Apply settings to new AutoShapes** check box, and click **OK**.

3. On the **Objects** toolbar, click the button of the shape you want (such as the Oval button), hold down the [Shift] key, and drag to create a shape.

4. Double-click the line (not its handle), and under **Line** on the **Colors and Lines** tab of the **Format AutoShape** dialog box, change the **Color** and **Weight** to what you want. Then click **OK**.

**To connect shapes, and then format the connection line, page 55**

1. Click the **AutoShapes** button on the **Objects** toolbar or point to **Picture** on the **Insert** menu, and then click **AutoShapes**.

2. On the detachable **AutoShapes** toolbar, point to **Connectors**, and then click the type of connector you want.

3. Point to the first shape you want to connect, and when blue handles appear, drag a line from the shape to another shape.

**To group shapes or design elements, page 56**

→ Select the items you want to group by holding down the [Shift] key as you click each one in turn. Then on the **Arrange** menu, click **Group**.

**To ungroup shapes or design elements, page 56**

→ Click the grouped object, and then click the **Ungroup Objects** button that appears.

**To insert a ready-made element from the Design Gallery into a publication, page 58**

1. Click the **Design Gallery Object** button on the **Objects** toolbar, or click **Design Gallery Object** on the **Insert** menu.

2. In the left pane of the Design Gallery, click the category you want, and in the right pane, click the object you want. Then click **Insert Object**.

# 3 Creating Colorful Cards and Calendars

**To create a folded card based on a layout template, page 69**

1. In the **Publication Types** list, click **Invitation Cards**. In the center pane, click the design you want.

2. Under **Customize** in the right pane, select the **Color scheme**, **Font scheme**, and **Business information**.

3. Under **Options**, select the **Page size** and **Layout** (if these options are available for the selected card design). Then click **Create**.

**To create a postcard, page 78**

1. In the **Publication Types** list, click **Postcards**. In the center pane, click the design you want.

2. Under **Customize** in the right pane, select the **Color scheme**, **Font scheme**, and **Business information**.

3. Under **Options**, select the **Page size** and **Side 2 information**. Then click **Create**.

**To merge a publication with a data source, page 79**

1. In the open publication, on the **Tools** menu, point to **Mailings and Catalogs**, and click **Mail Merge**.

2. With the **Use an existing list** option selected under **Create recipient list**, click **Next: Create or connect to a recipient list** at the bottom of the task pane.

3. In the **Select Data Source** dialog box, navigate to the recipient list you want, and double-click it.

4. In the **Select Table** dialog box, select the data you want, and then click **OK**.

5. In the **Mail Merge Recipients** dialog box, change any settings you want or use the default settings, and then click **OK**.

6. By clicking the links under **More Items** in the task pane, insert the fields you want to include in the merged publication.

7. At the bottom of the **Mail Merge** task pane, click **Next: Create merged publication**.

8. In the task pane, click **Merge to a new publication**. Then on the page sorter, click each page in turn to see the results.

### To create a calendar, page 88

1. In the **Publication Types** list, click **Calendars**. In the center pane, click the design you want.

2. In the right pane, under **Customize**, select the **Color scheme**, **Font scheme**, and **Business information**.

3. Under **Options**, select the **Page size** and **Timeframe**.

4. If you want to create a calendar for other than the current time period, click **Set Calendar Dates**, choose the time period, and then click **OK**.

5. If the **Include schedule of events** option is available and you want to create a smaller calendar that includes a text area for events or other information, select that check box.

6. Click **Create**.

### To replace an image, page 89

1. Right-click the existing picture, point to **Change Picture**, and then click **From File**.

2. In the **Insert Picture** dialog box, browse to and select the picture you want, and then click **Insert**.

### To switch between task panes, page 91

→ On the task pane title bar, click the **Other Task Panes** button, and then click the task pane you want to display.

### To apply a background to a publication, page 91

→ In the **Background** task pane, select the background color and gradient you want.

or

→ In the **Background** task pane, click **More backgrounds**, and then specify the gradient, texture, pattern, picture, and/or tint you want.

**To install the Microsoft Save As PDF Or XPS add-in, page 93**

1. Start your default Internet browser, and go to *office.microsoft.com/en-us/downloads/*.

2. In the left pane, under **By Version**, click **2007 Office System**, click **2007 Microsoft Office System**, and then click **Add-ins**.

3. In the list of add-ins, click **2007 Microsoft Office Add-in: Microsoft Save As PDF or XPS**.

4. On the installation page, click **Continue**. After the Genuine Advantage Tool confirms that you are running genuine, licensed software, click **Install** and follow the installation instructions given.

5. After the installation completes, navigate to the publication you want to submit to a printer, and then double-click it.

**To create a CD or file package containing all the files necessary to submit a publication to a professional printer, page 94**

1. On the **File** menu, point to **Pack and Go**, and then click **Take to a Commercial Printing Service**.

2. In the **Take to a Commercial Printing Service** task pane, click **Printing Options**.

3. In the **Print Options** dialog box, apply any settings necessary, and then click **OK**.

4. At the bottom of the task pane, click **Save**.

5. Insert a blank CD in your CD burner, and with **Burn to disc on D:\** (or the equivalent drive on your computer) selected, click **Next**. If your computer does not have a CD burner, select the Other Location option instead, and then browse to the folder in which you want to store the package.

6. When the wizard announces that your publication is successfully packed, clear the **Print a composite proof** check box, and then click **OK**.

# 4  Marketing Your Product, Service, or Organization

**To create an envelope, page 105**

1. In the **Publication Types** list, click **Envelopes**. In the center pane, click the design you want.

2. In the right pane, under **Customize**, select the **Color scheme**, **Font scheme**, and **Business information**.

3. Under **Options**, select the **Page size** and whether to include a logo image. Then click **Create**.

**To edit a logo and add it to the Content Library, page 106**

1. On the **Objects** toolbar, click the **Design Gallery Object** button, and in the left pane of the **Design Gallery**, click **Logos**. If necessary, enlarge the gallery window by dragging its border so you can see the logos in the center pane.

2. In the center pane, click the style of logo you want to create, set any other options necessary, and then click **Insert Object**.

3. Drag the logo to the area of the publication you want.

4. On the **Arrange** menu, click **Ungroup**, and then click a blank area of the publication to release the selection and enable editing of the individual logo elements.

5. Make any edits and add any images you want to the logo. Then select the elements in the logo (hold down the ⎵Shift⎵ key as you click each one), and group them.

**To add an object to the Content Library, page 107**

1. Right-click the object, and then click **Add to Content Library**.

2. In the **Add Item to Content Library** dialog box, enter a name for the object in the **Title** box.

3. If you want to assign the object to a category that doesn't appear in the **Categories** list, click the **Edit Category List** button, add, delete, or rename categories, and then click **OK**.

4. In the **Categories** list, select the check box of any category you want to assign the object to. Then click **OK**.

**To change the grid proportions, page 116**

1. On the **Arrange** menu, click **Layout Guides**, and then in the **Layout Guides** dialog box, click the **Grid Guides** tab.

2. Under **Column Guides**, change the **Columns** setting, and under **Row Guides**, change the **Rows** setting to what you want. Then click **OK**.

**To align objects, page 117**

→ Select the object or objects you want to align with each other or relative to the margin guides. Then on the **Arrange** menu, point to **Align or distribute**, and click the alignment or distribution option you want.

**To change the stacking order of an object, page 117**

→ Select the object you want to change the position of. Then on the **Arrange** menu, point to **Order**, and click the change of position you want.

**To create a text watermark, page 122**

1. Insert a text box, size it to span the page, and then rotate it to the angle you want.
2. Enter the watermark text in the text box, select the text, and set the font and size so that the text fills the box.
3. On the **Formatting** toolbar, click the **Font Color** arrow, and then click **Fill Effects**.
4. In the **Fill Effects** dialog box, set the **Base color** to the color you want. Then click one of the three lightest **Tint/Shade** boxes (10%, 20%, or 30%), and click **OK**.

**To create a graphic watermark, page 122**

→ Insert and size the graphic as usual. Then on the **Picture** toolbar, click the **Color** button, and in the list, click **Washout**.

**To link text boxes to flow text from one to the other, page 128**

1. Select the first text box you want to link. Then on the **Connect Text Boxes** toolbar, click the **Create Text Box Link** button.
2. Move the pointer over an empty text box, and when the pointer changes to a pouring pitcher, click the mouse button.

**To unlink text boxes, page 128**

→ Select the text box that has the forward link you want to remove. Then on the **Connect Text Boxes** toolbar, click the **Break Forward Link** button.

**To change the text wrapping style of a photograph, page 129**

1. Click the photograph, and then on the **Picture** toolbar, click the **Format Picture** button.
2. On the **Layout** tab of the **Format Picture** dialog box, under **Wrapping Style**, click the style you want, and then click **OK**.

# 5 Creating Text-Based Publications

**To replace placeholder text, page 138**

→ Click the placeholder text, and then enter the text you want.

**To automatically size text to fit the text box in which it appears, page 139**

→ Select the text box. Then on the **Format** menu, point to **AutoFit Text**, and click **Shrink Text On Overflow**.

**To add pages to a newsletter, page 141**

→ On the **Insert** menu, click **Duplicate Page** to insert a page with the same layout as the previous page.

or

1. On the **Insert** menu, click **Page**.

2. In the **Insert Newsletter Page** dialog box, in the **Available page types** list or in the **Left-hand page** and **Right-hand page** lists, click the page type you want to insert. Then click **OK**.

or

1. On the **Insert** menu, click **Page**. Then in the **Insert Newsletter Page** dialog box, click **More**.

2. In the **Insert Page** dialog box, select the number of pages to insert, the insertion location, and the page content. Then click **OK.**

**To apply or reapply a font theme to an existing publication, page 143**

→ Display the **Font Schemes** section of the **Format Publication** task pane. Then in the **Apply a font scheme** list, click the font scheme you want.

**To trace the continuation of a story in a newsletter, page 152**

→ Click the **Go to Previous Text Box** and **Go to Next Text Box** buttons.

**To move pages in a newsletter, page 153**

→ To move a two-page spread, in **Two-Page Spread** view, on the page sorter, drag either page to the new location.

→ To move one page, turn off **Two-Page Spread** view. Then on the page sorter, drag the page to the new location.

**To insert or remove Continued notices, page 153**

1. Select the text box. On the **Format** menu, click **Text Box**.

2. On the **Text Box** tab of the **Format Text Box** dialog box, clear or select the **Include "Continued on page..."** check box.

**To format text in columns, page 154**

→ Click the **Columns** button. Then in the **Columns** dialog box, set the number of columns you want, and click **OK**.

**To delete a page from a newsletter, page 157**

→ On the page sorter, right-click the page button of the page you want to delete, and click **Delete Page**. Then in the **Microsoft Office Publisher** message box, click **Yes** to confirm the deletion of the page, including the empty text box.

**To create a publication from a Microsoft Office Online template, page 164**

1. In the **Publication Types** list, click the publication type you want to search for.

2. In the center pane, under **Microsoft Office Online Templates**, click **View templates from Microsoft Office Online**.

3. Select a template you like, and then click **Create**.

**To edit a story by using Microsoft Office Word, page 165**

→ Right-click the main placeholder text, point to **Change Text**, and then click **Edit Story in Microsoft Word**.

**To check the spelling of a publication, page 166**

1. On the **Tools** menu, point to **Spelling**, and then click **Spelling**.

2. In the **Check Spelling** dialog box, correct any errors that appear, by accepting the suggestion or entering any replacement text you want in the **Change to** box. Then click **Change** to effect the replacement and move to the next detected error.

3. In the **Microsoft Office Publisher** dialog box that appears when the spelling check is complete, click **OK**.

# 6 Communicating Your Message Online

**To create an e-mail message from a template, page 172**

1. In the **Publication Types** list, click **E-mail**. In the center pane, click the design you want.

2. Under **Customize** in the right pane, select the **Color scheme**, **Font scheme**, and **Business information**. Then click **Create**.

**To select a group of objects, page 174**

→ On the **Objects** toolbar, click the **Select Objects** button. Then drag a box to encompass the objects you want to select.

**To view the source code of an e-mail message, page 175**

1. On the **File** menu, point to **Send E-mail**, and then click **E-mail Preview**.

2. Right-click the HTML page, and then click **View Source**. (If you're using a browser other than Windows Internet Explorer, click the equivalent command.)

**To send a publication as an e-mail message, page 176**

1. On the **File** menu, point to **Send E-mail**, and then click **Send as Message**.

2. If the **Send as Message** dialog box appears, click **Send all pages** or **Send current page only**, and then click **OK**.

3. If you have multiple e-mail accounts configured, select the account from which you want to send the message.

4. Address and send the message.

**To merge an e-mail message with a data source, page 178**

1. Open the e-mail publication. Then on the **Tools** menu, point to **Mailings and Catalogs**, and then click **E-mail Merge**.

2. In the **E-mail Merge** task pane, complete each of the following steps, clicking the **Next** link as you finish each step:

   a. Creating or connecting to the recipient list

   b. Preparing the publication

   c. Sending the merged publication

**To add a publication as a top-level page to a Web site, page 188**

1. Open the publication in Publisher. On the **File** menu, click **Publish to the Web**.

2. In the **Publish to the Web** dialog box, browse to your Web site directory structure, name the file, and then click **Save** to save an HTML version of the file.

3. Open the site in Publisher. Click anywhere on the navigation bar, and then click the **Navigation Bar Options** button that appears.

4. In the **Navigation Bar Properties** dialog box, click **Add Link**.

5. In the **Add Link** dialog box, in the **Link to** list, click **Existing File or Web Page**. Then in the **Look in** pane, browse to the HTML version of the file.

6. In the **Text to display** box, enter the text you want to appear on the navigation link. Then click **OK**.

7. To change the position of the linked file within the navigation link structure, click the **Move Up** and **Move Down** buttons. When the navigation links appear in the order you want, click **OK** in the **Navigation Bar Properties** dialog box.

**To create a Web site based on a template, page 189**

1. In the **Publication Types** list, click **Web Sites**. In the center pane, click the design you want.

2. Under **Customize** in the right pane, select the **Color scheme**, **Font scheme**, and **Business information**.

3. Under **Options**, select the **Navigation bar** location. Then click **Create**.

**To customize the navigation bar links, page 191**

1. Click anywhere on the navigation bar, and then click the **Navigation Bar Options** button that appears.

2. In the **Navigation Bar Properties** dialog box, in the **Links** list, click the link you want to move, and then click **Move Down** or **Move Up** until it's in the position you want.

**To configure a command button on a form, page 192**

1. Right-click the button, and then click **Format Form Properties**.

2. In the **Command Button Properties** dialog box, accept or change the button text. Then click **Form Properties**.

3. In the **Form Properties** dialog box, select the data retrieval method and the information appropriate to that method. Then click **OK** in each of the two open dialog boxes.

# Chapter at a Glance

Start new publications, **page 2**

Store personal and company information, **page 20**

Print publications, **page 23**

# 1 Getting Started with Publisher 2007

**In this chapter, you will learn to:**

✔ Start new publications.

✔ Save and close publications.

✔ Open and view publications.

✔ Store personal and company information.

✔ Print publications.

When you use a computer or typewriter to create text documents, you are *word processing*. When you use a specialized computer program to create professional-quality documents that combine text and other visual elements in non-linear arrangements, you are *desktop publishing*. Microsoft Office Publisher 2007 is designed specifically to handle the various desktop publishing needs of individuals and small organizations. Publisher makes it easy to efficiently create a wide range of *publications*, from simple flyers to complex brochures. Even novice users will be able to work productively in Publisher after only a brief introduction.

In this chapter, you will first learn various ways to create blank publications and publications based on existing content. You will save a publication, open an existing publication, and display different views of it. You will then store standard contact information in Publisher for later use. Finally, you will preview and print a publication.

**See Also** Do you need only a quick refresher on the topics in this chapter? See the Quick Reference entries on pages xxvii–xli.

**Important** Before you can use the practice files in this chapter, you need to install them from the book's companion CD to their default location. See "Using the Book's CD" on page xvii for more information.

> **Troubleshooting** Graphics and operating system–related instructions in this book reflect the Windows Vista user interface. If your computer is running Windows XP and you experience trouble following the instructions as written, please refer to the "Information for Readers Running Windows XP" section at the beginning of this book.

# Starting New Publications

When you first start Publisher, you see the Getting Started window, from which you can start a new publication or open an existing one.

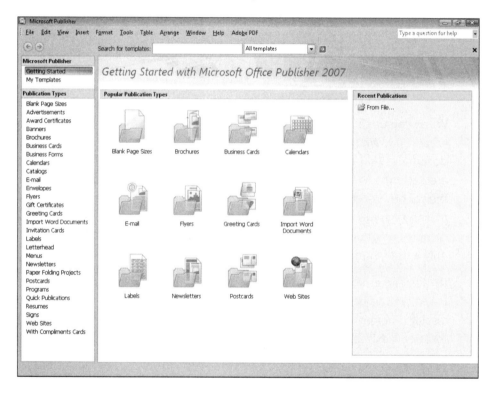

> **Important** What you see on your screen might not match the graphics in this book exactly. The screens in this book were captured at a resolution of 1024 × 768 pixels with the Windows Vista Basic color scheme. The Windows taskbar is hidden to increase the space available for the program window.

The Getting Started window provides several options for starting a new publication, such as the following:

- If you need help designing the publication *layout*, you can base the publication on one of the design *templates* that comes with Publisher. If none of these templates meets your needs, you can download a sample publication from *Microsoft Office Online* and then customize it. You can also base publications on your own custom templates.

  **See Also** For information about creating your own templates, see the sidebar titled "Custom Templates," later in this chapter.

  > **Tip** New publications are continually being added to Office Online, so visit the site occasionally to see what's new.

- If you have an existing publication that is close enough in content and design to be a good starting point, you can save a copy of that publication as the starting point for the new one.

- If your content is in a Microsoft Office Word document, you can import the document into Publisher and then lay out the text as you want it.

- If you want to manually design the publication, you can create a new blank publication and specify the page size you want.

  **See Also** For information about creating a blank publication, see "Formatting Text for Visual Impact" in Chapter 2, "Creating Visual Interest."

## Using a Template

Creating a publication from a blank page is time-consuming and requires quite a bit of design skill and knowledge about Publisher. Even people with intermediate and advanced Publisher skills can save time by capitalizing on the work someone else has already done. In the Getting Started window, you can choose a *publication type*, preview *thumbnails* of the available designs of that type, and experiment with different color schemes and font schemes.

> **Tip** The templates that come with Publisher, as well as those that are available from Office Online, have associated *keywords*. You can type a keyword in the Search For Templates box at the top of the Getting Started window and then click the Search button (the green arrow to the right of the search location list) to display thumbnails of templates to which that keyword has been assigned.

When you create a publication based on a template, you are not opening the actual template file; instead, you are creating a new file that includes all the *placeholders*, graphic elements, and formatting of the template. You customize the publication with your own information, typing text and placing graphics and other elements in the placeholders provided. The new file is temporary until you save it.

**See Also** For information about saving a publication, see "Saving and Closing Publications," later in this chapter.

## Importing a Word Document

To import the text of a Word document into a publication, you click Import Word Documents in the Publication Types list and then choose a document design, page size, and column layout. (If you prefer, you can forego the design and choose only a generic page size or a paper format such as those available from Avery.) Publisher converts the document and inserts it into a new publication, adding as many pages as necessary to hold the complete document. You can then add a title and replace any other placeholders that are part of the design, or you can add new elements to suit the purpose of the publication.

In this exercise, you will create a publication based on a ready-made template that comes with Publisher. You will also import a Word document.

> **USE** the *Importing* document. This practice file is located in the *Documents\Microsoft Press\SBS_Publisher2007\GettingStarted* folder.

Start

1. Click the **Start** button, click **All Programs**, click **Microsoft Office**, and then click **Microsoft Office Publisher 2007**.

   The Getting Started window opens.

2. In the left pane of the Getting Started window, under **Publication Types**, click **Quick Publications**.

   > **Tip** If you are already working on a publication, you can display the Getting Started window by clicking New on the File menu (but not by clicking the New button on the Standard toolbar).

Under the publication type heading at the top of the center pane is a list of template categories for the selected publication type, followed by a link to the templates of this type that are available from Office Online. (Clicking the link displays the online templates under the Microsoft Office Online Templates heading rather than opening a separate Internet browser window.) Thumbnails of the available publication templates appear in category order. The right pane displays a larger thumbnail of the selected template, and any available customization options.

3. In the category list at the top of the center pane, click **Classic Designs**.

   The pane scrolls to display thumbnails of the ready-made classic designs for one-page announcements or cover pages.

4. Scroll the center pane to see the available designs, and then under **Classic Designs**, click the **Pixel** thumbnail.

The selected publication is indicated by an orange frame. A larger thumbnail and the customization options that you can set before you create the publication appear in the right pane.

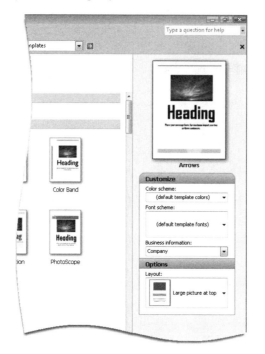

5. In the right pane, under **Options**, click the **Layout** arrow (to the right of the **Large picture at top** setting), and then in the list, click **Large picture in the middle**.

   All the thumbnails change to show this layout option.

6. In the lower-right corner of the window, click **Create**.

   A publication based on the selected template opens in a new Publisher program window.

---

**Tip** You can create a simple publication directly from a Word document. On the Standard toolbar, click the Open button. Then with All Publisher Files selected as the file type in the Open Publication dialog box, locate and double-click the Word document you want to use. The new publication contains the document text but doesn't have a template applied.

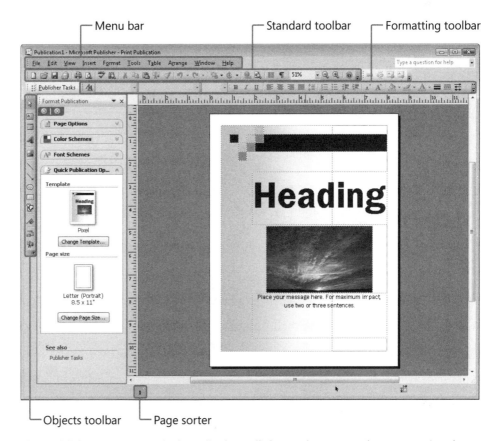

Menu bar — Standard toolbar — Formatting toolbar

Objects toolbar — Page sorter

The Publisher program window displays all the tools you need to customize the publication. You carry out most tasks by clicking commands on menus or buttons on toolbars. Common tasks you might want to perform for the current publication are gathered in one convenient place in the Format Publication task pane to the left of the publication workspace.

**See Also** For information about menu commands and toolbar buttons, see "Introducing Publisher 2007" at the beginning of this book.

**7.** In the **Format Publication** task pane, under **Quick Publication Options**, click **Change Template**.

Publisher opens the Change Template window, which looks very similar to the Getting Started window. You can apply a different Quick Publication template to the open publication, or you can switch to an entirely different type of publication.

8. In the center pane, click **Layers**, and then click **OK**.

   The fonts, colors, and arrangement of the existing content change to reflect the new template.

9. Minimize the Publication1 window to redisplay the **Publication Types** list in the original Getting Started window.

> **Tip**  If the Getting Started window is closed, you can click New on the File menu of the Publication1 window to open it in a separate program window.

10. In the **Publication Types** list, click **Import Word Documents**. Then in the center pane, under **Classic Designs**, click **Capsules**.

11. Under **Options** in the right pane, click the **Columns** arrow, and then click **2**.

    All the thumbnails change to show a two-column layout.

12. Select the **Include title page** check box, and then click **Create**.

    Publisher opens the Import Word Document dialog box so that you can designate the document whose text you want to use.

> **Troubleshooting** This graphic shows the Import Word Document dialog box that opens on a computer running Windows Vista. If your computer is running Windows XP, navigational dialog boxes such as this one will look and work differently. For more information, refer to the "Information for Readers Running Windows XP" section at the beginning of this book.

**13.** In your *Documents* folder, navigate to the *Microsoft Press\SBS_Publisher2007\ GettingStarted* folder, and double-click the *Importing* document.

Publisher creates a new publication based on the Capsules template that contains the text of the *Importing* document.

**14.** On the *page sorter* at the bottom of the program window, click the page **2** button.

Publisher has inserted the contents of the imported Word document in two columns on the second page.

> **BE SURE TO** leave the publications open for use in the next exercise.

# Saving and Closing Publications

When you create a new publication, it exists only in your computer's temporary memory until you save it. Even if you will never use a particular publication again, you might want to save it so that you can use it later as the basis for a similar publication.

## Saving a New Publication

The first time you save a publication, you can click the Save button on the Standard toolbar or click Save or Save As on the File menu. Either action opens the Save As dialog box, where you can assign a name and choose a storage location.

In Publisher, the dialog boxes that allow you to navigate to a particular storage location, such as the Save As and Open dialog boxes, are linked. If this is the first time in this Publisher session that you have used one of these dialog boxes, it displays the contents of your *Documents* folder. Subsequently, it displays the contents of whatever folder you last used. You use standard Windows techniques to navigate to or create other folders.

**See Also**  For information about navigating in Windows Vista, refer to *Windows Vista Step by Step* by Joan Preppernau and Joyce Cox (Microsoft Press, 2007).

After you save a publication for the first time, you can save changes simply by clicking the Save button on the Standard toolbar. The new version of the publication then overwrites the previous version.

> **Tip**  By default, Publisher saves the publication you are working on every 10 minutes, in case the program stops responding or your computer shuts down unexpectedly. To adjust the time interval between saves, click Options on the Tools menu in an open publication, click the Save tab, and change the Save AutoRecover setting to the interval you want.

## Saving a Different Version of the Same Publication

If you want to keep both a new version of a publication and the original version, click Save As on the File menu and save a new version with a different name in the same location or with the same name in a different location. (You cannot have two files with the same name in the same folder.) When you save a new version of a publication in this way, the new version is active in Publisher, and the original version is not.

If you want to be sure you can return to a previous version of a publication if you don't like the results of changes you make, you can save a backup of the publication. Instead of clicking Save in the Save As dialog box, click the Save arrow and then click Save With Backup. Publisher saves a separate copy of the publication in the same folder.

## Closing a Publication

If more than one publication is open, you can close the active publication by clicking the Close button at the right end of the title bar. If only one publication is open, clicking the Close button closes the publication and also quits Publisher. If you want to close the publication but leave Publisher open, you must click Close on the File menu. Publisher then displays the Getting Started window so that you can choose another publication to work on.

> **Tip** If you have several publications open and you want to quit Publisher, you don't have to close the publications first. You can simply click Exit on the File menu.

In this exercise, you will save a new publication in a new folder. Then you will save the same publication with the same name in a different folder.

**USE** the publications you created in the previous exercise.

1. Display the two-page publication based on the *Importing* document.
2. On the **Standard** toolbar, click the **Save** button.

Save

   The Save As dialog box opens. In the File Name box, Word suggests a possible name for this file.

Navigation Pane

Display or hide the Navigation Pane by clicking Browse Folders or Hide Folders.

3. If your **Save As** dialog box does not display the **Navigation Pane**, click the **Browse Folders** button.

   You can now easily navigate to different locations, change the folder view, and create new folders.

4. If the contents of your *GettingStarted* folder are not displayed, click **Documents** in the **Favorite Links** list. Then in your *Documents* folder, navigate to the *Microsoft Press\SBS_Publisher2007\GettingStarted* folder.

5. Replace the suggested name in the **File name** box with SeriesProposal, and then click **Save**.

> **Troubleshooting** Programs that run on the Windows operating systems use file name extensions to identify different types of files. For example, the extension *.pub* identifies Publisher documents. Windows Vista programs do not display these extensions by default, and you shouldn't type them in the Save As dialog box. When you save a file, Publisher automatically adds the extension associated with the file type selected in the Save As Type box.

Notice that *SeriesProposal* now appears in the publication title bar. From now on, you can click the Save button any time you want to quickly save changes to this file. Publisher already knows the name of this file, so instead of asking you to name the file, it simply overwrites the previous version with the new version.

6. On the **File** menu, click **Save As**, and then on the dialog box's toolbar, click the **New Folder** button.

7. Type My Publications as the name of the new folder, and then press ⌨Enter.

   *My Publications* is now the current folder in the Save As dialog box.

8. Click **Save**.

   The Save As dialog box closes, and Publisher saves the *SeriesProposal* file in the *My Publications* folder. You now have two versions of the document saved with the same name but in different folders.

9. On the menu bar, click the **Window** menu.

   At the bottom of the menu is a list of the currently open publications.

10. Click **Publication1** in the list to display the one-page publication you created earlier in this chapter.

11. Click the **Close** button at the right end of the Publisher program window title bar to close the publication without saving it.

> **Troubleshooting** If Publisher asks whether you want to save changes when you close the publication, click No.

12. On the **File** menu, click **Close** to close the *SeriesProposal* publication without quitting Publisher.

## Custom Templates

If you create a special publication layout that you might want to use for future pub-lications, you can save the publication as a custom template and then use it as the basis for new publications as you would a built-in template.

To save a publication as a template:

1. On the **File** menu, click **Save As**.

2. In the **File name** box of the **Save As** dialog box, type a name for the template.

3. Click the **Save as type** arrow, and then in the list, click **Publisher Template**.

   Publisher displays your default *Templates* folder.

> **Important** For a template to be available from the My Templates page, it must be stored in the default *Templates* folder. If you store a template in a different folder, you can browse to that folder and double-click the template file to open a new publica-tion based on the template.

4. If you want to assign the template to a specific category, click the **Change** button. Select the category from the list or select the current category and type the name of a new category. Then click **OK**.

5. Click **Save**.

In the My Templates window, you can change the category of a template or delete it by pointing to the template, clicking the arrow that appears, and then clicking the command.

To create a new publication based on the custom template:

1. In the left pane of the Getting Started window, under **Microsoft Publisher**, click **My Templates**.

   The My Templates page displays templates stored in the default Templates folder, organized by category.

2. In the center pane, click the template you want, and then click **Create**.

   Publisher opens a new publication based on your custom template.

The simplest way to change a custom template after you save it is to create a publica-tion based on the template, make the changes, and then save the revised publication as a template with the original template name, overwriting the old one.

# Opening and Viewing Publications

How you open an existing publication depends on what you are doing in Publisher at the time. You can open a publication in many ways, most of which will be familiar to you from other 2007 Microsoft Office system programs:

● In the Getting Started window, you can click a publication you have recently worked on in the Recent Publications pane on the right side of the window.

● If the publication you want to work with is not listed in the Recent Publications pane, you can click From File at the top of the pane to display the Open Publication dialog box.

● If you are working on one publication and want to open another, you can click the Open button on the Standard toolbar or click Open on the File menu to display the Open Publication dialog box.

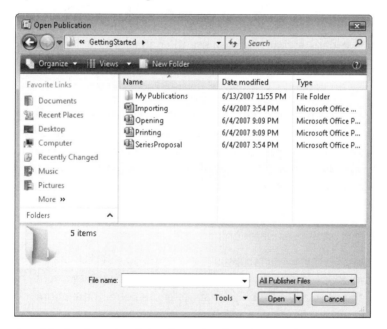

As with the Save As dialog box, the first time you use the Open Publication dialog box in a Publisher session, the dialog box displays the contents of your *Documents* folder. To see the contents of a different folder, you use standard Windows techniques. After you locate the file you want to work with, you can double-click it to open it, or you can click it and then click Open in the lower-right corner of the dialog box.

Clicking a file name and then clicking the Open arrow displays a list of alternative ways to open the selected file. To open a publication without the risk of making inadvertent changes, you can open the file as *read-only*. You can make changes to a read-only publication, but you will have to save the edited publication with a different name or in a different location.

● If you intend to distribute a publication electronically—for example, via e-mail or through a Web site—you can open the publication in your default Web browser by clicking the Open arrow and then clicking Open In Browser.

## Changing the View

You need to know how to move around in a publication so that you can view parts of a publication that don't fit in the window, and so that you can edit its text. If a page of a publication is bigger than the window, you can bring hidden parts into view by changing the zoom level or scrolling the page, in much the same way that you do in other Windows programs. If you want to display a specific page of a publication, or display a two-page spread, you can use the page sorter at the bottom of the window.

**See Also**  For information about manipulating pages from the page sorter, see "Creating Newsletters" in Chapter 5, "Creating Text-Based Publications."

Publisher displays full pages at a 50 to 60 percent zoom level, depending on your screen resolution and the page size. At this magnification, it can be difficult to accurately edit text and place visual elements. So you need to know how to zoom in for a closer look at a particular element and then zoom out again to get an overview of the entire page. With Publisher, you can zoom in and out in several ways, such as the following:

● To zoom in and out by set increments, you can click the Zoom In and Zoom Out buttons on the Standard toolbar.

● To select a specific percentage from a list, you can click the Zoom arrow on the Standard toolbar or click a Zoom command on the View menu. You can also change the magnification so that the entire page or the entire width of the page fits in the window.

● To zoom to a non-standard percentage, you can click the current entry in the Zoom box and type the percentage you want.

● To zoom in on a specific element, you can click the element, click the Zoom arrow, and then click Selected Objects.

In this exercise, you will open an existing publication, move from page to page, and then change the zoom level to suit your needs.

**USE** the *Opening* publication. This practice file is located in the *Documents\Microsoft Press\ SBS_Publisher2007\GettingStarted* folder.

**BE SURE TO** close any open publications and display the Getting Started window before beginning this exercise.

1. In the **Recent Publications** pane of the **Getting Started** window, click **From File**.

   The Open Publication dialog box opens, showing the contents of the folder you used for your last open or save action.

2. If the contents of the *GettingStarted* folder are not displayed, click **Documents** in the **Favorite Links** list. Then in your *Documents* folder, navigate to the *Microsoft Press\SBS_Publisher2007\GettingStarted* folder.

3. Double-click the *Opening* publication to open it.

Close

4. At the right end of the **Format Publication** task pane title bar, click the **Close** button to close the task pane.

5. Move the mouse pointer over the elements of the cover page of the publication, pausing on each until a ScreenTip identifying the element type appears.

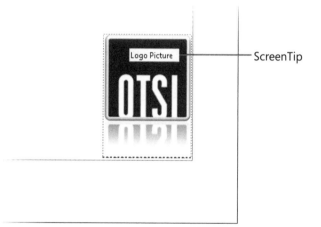

In a publication that has many elements, you can use these ScreenTips to identify the part you want to work with.

6. On the page sorter at the bottom of the window, click the page **2** button.

   Publisher displays pages 2 and 3 of the publication.

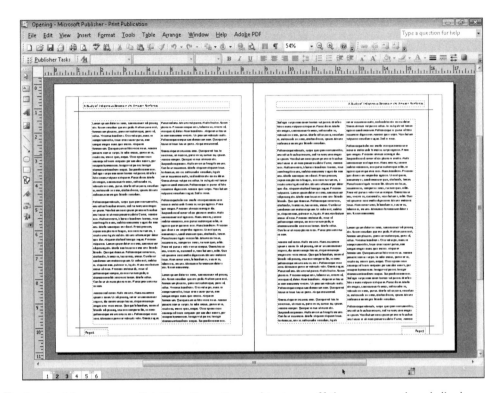

7. On the **View** menu, click **Two-Page Spread** to turn off the command and display only the selected page.

> **Tip** When people read a printed publication, they see a *spread* consisting of facing left and right pages. While you work on a publication that has more than two pages, you might want to view it in Two-Page Spread view to ensure that elements on the left and right pages are balanced.

8. On the page sorter, click the page **5** button to display the penultimate page of the publication.

> **Tip** Because all elements of a publication are contained in frames, you cannot move to the beginning or end of a publication by pressing Ctrl+Enter or Ctrl+End as you can in other Office system programs. However, those key combinations will take you to the beginning or end of the text in the active frame.

9. Click the image in the center of the page, click the **Zoom** arrow on the **Standard** toolbar, and then click **Selected Objects**.

Zoom

> **Troubleshooting**  Selected Objects appears in the Zoom list only when an object is selected.

Publisher magnifies the publication so that the image occupies the entire window.

Zoom Out

**10.** On the **Standard** toolbar, click the **Zoom Out** button repeatedly, until the **Zoom** box shows **100%**.

> **Tip**  To quickly switch between the current view and the actual-size view (100%), press the F9 key.

**11.** Click the **Zoom** arrow, and then click **Whole Page**.

Publisher restores the view to the original Zoom percentage.

 **CLOSE** the *Opening* publication without saving your changes.

## Multiple Open Publications

Publisher displays each publication you open in its own program window. You can switch from one open publication to another by clicking the Window menu and then clicking the name of the publication you want to work with at the bottom of the menu, or by clicking the publication's Windows taskbar button.

If you want to view all the open publications at the same time, you can click either Arrange All or Cascade on the Window menu:

● The Arrange All command divides your screen space vertically and horizontal-ly as necessary to display a tiled view of all the publication windows. This view is ideal for comparing two publications or for moving or copying elements from one publication to another.

● The Cascade command layers the publication windows so that all of their title bars are visible but you can see only the publication at the top of the stack. You can bring a different publication to the top of the stack by clicking its title bar.

# Storing Personal and Company Information

Many of the publications you create by using Publisher will include the same personal or company information, such as a name, an address, and a phone number. Instead of having to enter this information for each new publication, you enter it only once, in an *information set*. Then whenever a new publication includes an item from the information set, Publisher automatically pulls it from the stored record and plugs it in. Similarly, to update personal or company information throughout the publication, you need only update it once, in the information set.

In this exercise, you will create two information sets and apply them to a publication.

> **USE** the *Logo* publication. This practice file is located in the *Documents\Microsoft Press\ SBS_Publisher2007\GettingStarted* folder.
>
> **BE SURE TO** close any open publications and display the Getting Started window before beginning this exercise.

1. In the **Publication Types** list, click **Business Cards**, and then under **Newer Designs**, double-click **Marker**.

   Publisher creates a business card containing placeholders for standard information.

2. On the **Edit** menu, click **Business Information**.

   The Create New Business Information Set dialog box opens.

Publisher fills in any information already available on your computer.

> **Troubleshooting**  This dialog box appears only if you have not previously created an information set. If you already have an existing information set, the Business Information dialog box appears. Click New in this dialog box to display the Create New Business Information Set dialog box.

**3.**  Fill in the information in all the boxes other than the Logo box. If any information does not apply, delete it.

For example, if you are filling in personal information, delete the entries in the Job Position Or Title and Organization Name boxes and remove the logo.

**4.**  Below the **Logo** box, click **Change**.

The Insert Picture dialog box opens. You navigate in this dialog box the same way you do in the Save As or Open dialog box.

**5.**  Navigate to the *Documents\Microsoft Press\SBS_Publisher2007\GettingStarted* folder, and then double-click the *Logo* file.

The selected logo appears in the Logo preview area.

**6.**  In the **Business Information set name** box at the bottom of the dialog box, replace **Custom 1** with a name that represents the information you just entered, and then click **Save**.

For example, you might enter *Company* or *Personal*.

**7.**  In the **Business Information** dialog box, review the information you just entered, and then click **Update Publication**.

The business card now appears with your information in place.

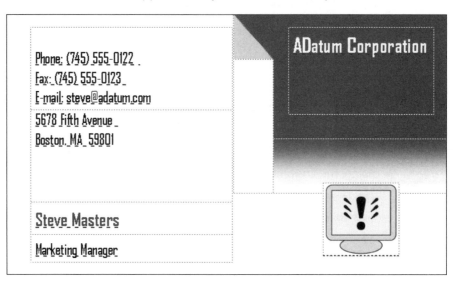

8. At the right end of the **Format Publication** task pane title bar, click the arrow, and then in the task pane list, click **Business Information**.

9. At the bottom of the task pane, click **Change Business Information** to display the **Business Information** dialog box.

> **Tip** From the Business Information dialog box, you can create, edit, or delete information sets.

10. Click **New**, and then in the **Create New Business Information Set** dialog box, enter a different set of information, again deleting any elements that are not relevant.

   For example, if you previously entered your company information, you might want to enter personal information this time.

11. In the **Business Information set name** box, type an appropriate name, and then click **Save**.

12. Close the dialog box without updating the business card publication, and then close the **Business Information** task pane.

13. On the **Edit** menu, click **Business Information**.

14. In the **Business Information** dialog box, click the arrow to the right of the box containing the name of the information set applied to the publication, click the name of the second set you created, and then click **Update Publication**.

Publisher updates the business card publication to reflect the information set you selected.

**✕ CLOSE** the publication without saving your changes.

**Tip** After you insert an item into a publication from the information set, you can add to it or delete parts of it without affecting the way it is stored in the information set. Similarly, if an item such as a tagline or motto is not included in the information set, you can replace the corresponding placeholder in a publication with text without affecting the saved information set.

# Printing Publications

When you are ready to print a publication, you can print to your computer's default printer and with the default settings by clicking the Print button on the Standard toolbar. To use a different printer or change the print settings, click Print on the File menu to open the Print dialog box. You can then specify which printer to use, what to print, and how many copies, and you can make other changes to the print settings.

## Previewing a Publication

Before you print a publication, you will almost always want to check how it will look on paper by previewing it. Previewing is essential for multi-page publications but is helpful even for one-page publications. In this view, Publisher shows exactly how each page of the publication will look when printed and displays a Print Preview toolbar to provide tools for checking each page.

**Tip** Tools are unavailable on this toolbar if they are not relevant to your printer. For example, the Color/Grayscale button is unavailable if you don't have a color printer.

## Using Advanced Printer Settings

Usually the simple settings on the Publications And Paper Settings tab of the Print dialog box will meet your needs. If you have some experience with graphic design and have worked with a graphics program or a different desktop publishing program, you might want to use Publisher's advanced printer settings. If you don't have this type of experience, you can skip this section and move on to the printing exercise.

Clicking the Printer Details tab in the Print dialog box and then clicking Advanced Printer Setup displays a dialog box where you can adjust the following settings:

- On the Separations tab, you can change the output from Composite RGB to Composite Grayscale, Composite CMYK, or Separations. (To output composite CMYK or separations, your printer and printer driver must both be set to support PostScript language level 2 or later.) You can also change the resolution and half-tone screen settings.

- On the Page Settings tab, you will find settings for output orientation, bleeds, and printer's marks, including crop marks and color bars.

- On the Graphics And Fonts tab, you can allow or prevent font substitution, set the resolution or turn off the printing of pictures, and set downsampling rates for pictures and line art.

- On the Printer Setup Wizard tab, you can set up the paper orientation for manually feeding pages that you want to print on both sides, as well as the orientation for feeding envelopes.

When you want to print only a few copies of a publication, using your own printer is quick and easy. If you need many copies, you will often save time and money by going to a copy shop or commercial printer.

**See Also** For information about using a commercial printer to print a publication, see the sidebar titled "Ink and Paper" in Chapter 3, "Creating Colorful Cards and Calendars."

In this exercise, you will preview and then print a publication.

> **USE** the *Printing* publication. This practice file is located in the *Documents\Microsoft Press\SBS_Publisher2007\GettingStarted* folder.
> **BE SURE TO** install a printer and turn it on before starting this exercise.
> **OPEN** the *Printing* publication.

Print Preview

**1.** On the **Standard** toolbar, click the **Print Preview** button.

Publisher displays the Preview window and the Print Preview toolbar.

Multiple Pages

**2.** On the **Print Preview** toolbar, click the **Multiple Pages** button, and then in the grid, click the second thumbnail in the top row.

Publisher displays the first two pages of the publication side by side.

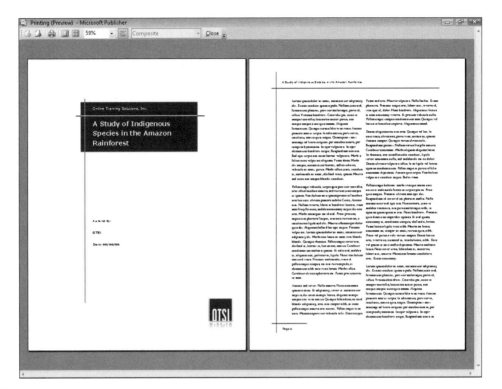

Page Down

3. On the **Print Preview** toolbar, click the **Page Down** button.

The next two pages appear. Note that in Print Preview, pages are not specifically displayed in spreads.

4. Move the pointer over page 3, and when the pointer changes to a magnifying glass, click the mouse button.

Publisher displays the part of page 3 that you clicked at a Zoom percentage of 100%.

5. Without moving the pointer, click again.

Publisher redisplays the two pages side by side.

Page Up

6. On the **Page Preview** toolbar, click the **Page Up** button to return to page 1. Then click **Close**.

7. On the page sorter at the bottom of the window, click page **2**. Then on the **File** menu, click **Print**.

The Print dialog box opens. The Preview box shows how the first page of the publication will look when it is printed.

> **Important** Because publications are usually carefully laid out before they are printed, it is unlikely that you will want to change settings such as the paper size and orientation in the Print dialog box. Instead you should change them in the Format Publication task pane or in the Page Setup dialog box so that you can see the effects on your publication before you print it.

**8.** If you have more than one printer available and you want to switch printers, click the **Printer name** arrow, and in the list, click the printer you want.

**9.** Under **Page Range**, click the **Current Page** option.

Because you selected page 2 before displaying the Print dialog box, the Preview box now displays page 2 as it will look when printed.

**10.** Under **Copies**, change the **Number of copies** setting to **2**, and then click **OK**.

Publisher prints two copies of the second page of the publication on the designated printer. To print specific pages, you would click the Pages option and then specify the pages—for example, enter 2-4 to print pages 2, 3, and 4; or enter 2,4 to print only pages 2 and 4.

> **Tip** When you print multiple copies of the entire publication, you can choose to have Publisher collate the copies (print one entire set of pages before printing the next) or print the publication on both sides of the paper.

**CLOSE** the *Printing* document without saving your changes, and if you are not continuing directly on to the next chapter, quit Publisher.

# Key Points

- From the Getting Started window, you can create a publication based on one of the many purpose-specific templates that come with Publisher. You can specify fonts, colors, and layout options before creating the publication.

- Publisher doesn't have multiple views, but because publications often consist of many different elements, it is important to know how to zoom in and out to check details or to get an overview of the entire publication.

- You can store sets of personal and company information for Publisher to automatically enter in all the appropriate places in your publications.

# Chapter at a Glance

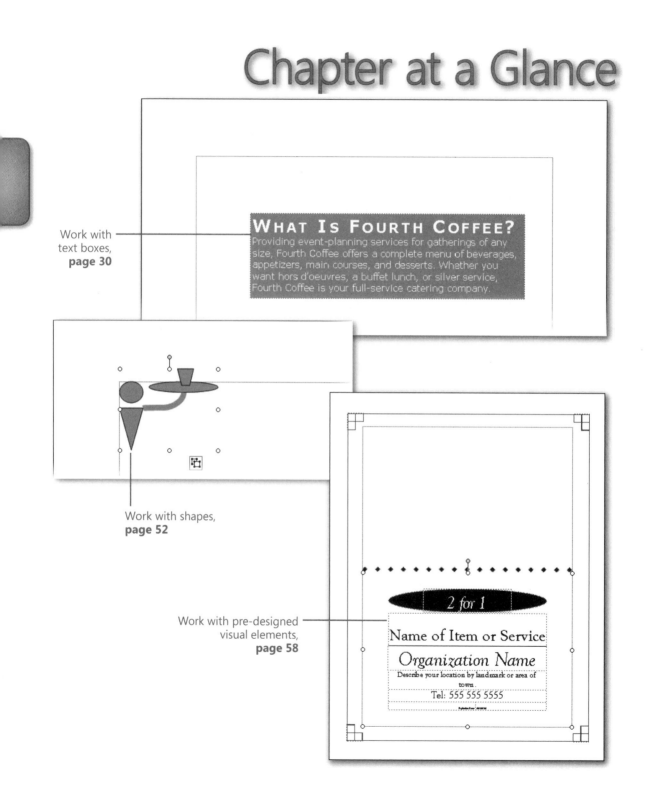

Work with
text boxes,
**page 30**

**WHAT IS FOURTH COFFEE?**
Providing event-planning services for gatherings of any size, Fourth Coffee offers a complete menu of beverages, appetizers, main courses, and desserts. Whether you want hors d'oeuvres, a buffet lunch, or silver service, Fourth Coffee is your full-service catering company.

Work with shapes,
**page 52**

Work with pre-designed
visual elements,
**page 58**

2 for 1

Name of Item or Service

Organization Name

Describe your location by landmark or area of town.

Tel: 555 555 5555

# 2 Creating Visual Interest

**In this chapter, you will learn to:**

✔ Work with text boxes.

✔ Work with WordArt.

✔ Work with graphics.

✔ Work with shapes.

✔ Work with pre-designed visual elements.

Microsoft Office Publisher 2007 is specifically designed to make it easy to create publications that contain a mixture of text and visual elements arranged in frames on the page. Knowing basic techniques for inserting and manipulating visual elements is the key to quickly assembling impressive publications.

The publications you create are most effective when you achieve the balance of text and graphics that best conveys your message. Some publications convey information through text and include visual elements only to catch the reader's eye or to reinforce or illustrate a point. At the other end of the scale, some publications include almost no text and instead rely on visual elements to carry the message.

In this chapter, you will first create a text object and see how to enhance the text with color and formatting. Then you will use WordArt to create fancy, stylized text for those occasions when regular formatting doesn't quite meet your needs. Next, you will insert clip art graphics and pictures, add borders, and change the size, color, and position of the images. You will draw, connect, and group shapes. Finally, you will insert ready-made design elements from the Design Gallery. The instructions in the exercises assume that you are working in a blank publication so that you can focus on the techniques you are learning. However, you can easily adapt the instructions to any type of publication.

**See Also** Do you need only a quick refresher on the topics in this chapter? See the Quick Reference entries on pages xxvii–xli.

> **Important** Before you can use the practice files in this chapter, you need to install them from the book's companion CD to their default location. See "Using the Book's CD" on page xvii for more information.

> **Troubleshooting** Graphics and operating system–related instructions in this book reflect the Windows Vista user interface. If your computer is running Windows XP and you experience trouble following the instructions as written, please refer to the "Information for Readers Running Windows XP" section at the beginning of this book.

# Working with Text Boxes

When you create a document by using a word processing program such as Microsoft Office Word 2007, you enter text on the page in the area defined by the margins. When you create a publication by using Publisher, however, you enter each section of text in a *text box*. You can create text boxes or manipulate the text boxes that are part of a Publisher template. The text box is an *object* that can be sized to fit the text it contains. You can type text directly into the text box, paste text from another file, or insert the entire contents of another file.

In Publisher, the text in a text box is called a *story*.  A story is any discrete block of text that occupies a single text box or a set of linked text boxes. It can be a single paragraph or multiple paragraphs.

**See Also**  For information about linking text boxes, see "Solving Organization Problems" in Chapter 5, "Creating Text-Based Publications."

## Manipulating a Text Box

After you create a text box, or when you click a text box to make it active, you can move it by dragging its *frame*.

> **Tip** To copy a text box, hold down the Ctrl key while you drag it.

You can drag the *handles* of the frame to change the size or shape of the box. If you want a specific size or shape, you can change the settings on the Size page of the Format Text Box dialog box. In this dialog box, you can also specify the following:

● The background color of the text box, whether it has a border, and the color of the border.

- The position of the text box on the page, and how text in adjacent frames flows around this text box.

- The vertical text alignment, the margins, and whether Publisher can automatically adjust the size of the text box to fit the amount of text you insert in it.

When a text box is active, a green *rotating handle* is attached to its upper-middle handle. You can drag this handle to change the angle of the text box and the text within it.

> **Tip** You can change the direction of text within the text box from horizontal to vertical by clicking the Rotate Text Within AutoShape By 90º option on the Text Box page of the Format Text Box dialog box. You can rotate the entire box by clicking Rotate Or Flip on the Arrange menu and then selecting one of the options.

## Formatting Text for Visual Impact

Brief splashes of text, such as those on a postcard or in a flyer, need to have more visual impact than longer blocks of text, such as those in a newsletter. You can vary the look of text by changing the *character formatting*:

- All text is displayed in a particular *font* consisting of alphabetic characters, numbers, and symbols that share a common design.

- Almost every font comes in a range of *font sizes*, which are measured in *points* from the top of letters that have parts that stick up (ascenders), such as *h*, to the bottom of letters that have parts that drop down (descenders), such as *p*. A point is approximately 1/72 of an inch.

- Almost every font comes in a range of *font styles*. The most common are regular (or plain), italic, bold, and bold italic.

- Fonts can be enhanced by applying *font effects*, such as underlining, small capital letters (small caps), or shadows.

- A palette of harmonious *font colors* is available, and you can also specify custom colors.

- You can alter the *character spacing* by pushing characters apart or squeezing them together.

In this exercise, you will create a blank publication, add a text box, and then insert the contents of an existing Word document. You will then format the text box by filling it with color and format the text by changing its character formatting.

**USE** the *Text* document. This practice file is located in the *Documents\Microsoft Press\ SBS_Publisher2007\VisualInterest* folder.

1. On the **Start** menu, click **All Programs**, click **Microsoft Office**, and then click **Microsoft Office Publisher 2007**.

2. In the **Publication Types** list, click **Blank Page Sizes**.

3. In the **Blank Page Sizes** pane, under **Standard**, click the **Letter (Portrait)** thumbnail. Then click **Create**.

> **Tip** If a publication is open, you can create a new blank publication by clicking the New button on the Standard toolbar.

Publisher creates a blank publication of the selected size. Blue *margin guides* designate the margins of the publication, which by default are set to 1 inch on all sides. To the left is the Format Publication task pane, and docked on the left side of the window is the Objects toolbar.

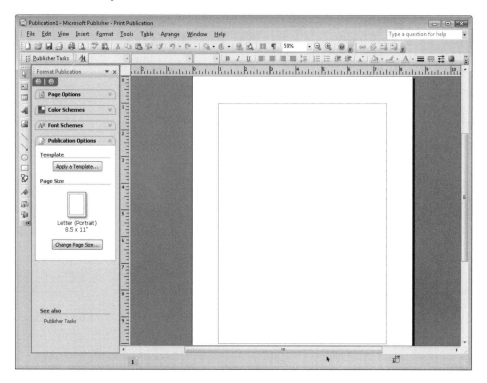

> **Tip** Throughout this chapter, we work with letter-size publications, but you can choose any size you want. You might want to try a different size for each exercise to see some of the available options.

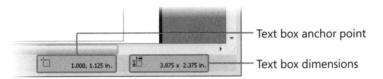

**Text Box**

4. Close the **Format Publication** task pane. Then on the **Objects** toolbar, click the **Text Box** button.

5. Move the cross-hair pointer over the blank page, and when the pointer is slightly to the right of the left margin guide and slightly below the top margin guide, hold down the mouse button, and drag to the right and down, without releasing the mouse button.

Notice as you drag that Publisher displays the exact *coordinates* of the upper-left corner (the anchor point) of the text box and its exact dimensions on the status bar. The anchor point coordinates are expressed in relation to the upper-left corner of the page.

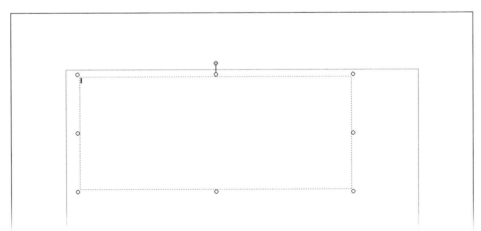

    1.000, 1.125 in.    — Text box anchor point

    3.875 x 2.375 in.    — Text box dimensions

6. Release the mouse button when the text box dimensions are **5.000 x 2.000 in**.

A blinking insertion point in the text box shows where any text you type will appear.

7. Without clicking anything else, on the **Insert** menu, click **Text File**.

   The Insert Text dialog box opens, displaying the contents of your *Documents* folder.

   **See Also** For information about how to move around in dialog boxes such as this one, see "Saving and Closing Publications" in Chapter 1, "Getting Started with Publisher 2007."

8. Navigate to the *Documents\Microsoft Press\SBS_Publisher2007\VisualInterest* folder, and double-click the *Text* document.

   Publisher inserts the contents of the document into the text box.

9. On the **Standard** toolbar, click the **Zoom** arrow, and change the zoom level to **100%**.

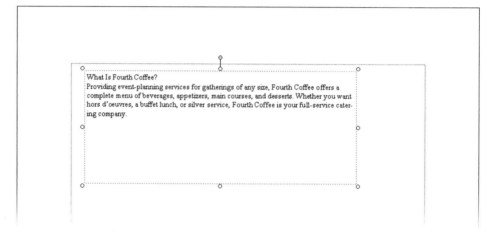

What Is Fourth Coffee?
Providing event-planning services for gatherings of any size, Fourth Coffee offers a complete menu of beverages, appetizers, main courses, and desserts. Whether you want hors d'oeuvres, a buffet lunch, or silver service, Fourth Coffee is your full-service catering company.

10. Point to the frame around the text box, and when the pointer changes to a four-headed arrow, drag the frame down and to the right, releasing the mouse button when the text box coordinates are **2.000, 2.000 in**.

   **Tip** Publisher can display measurements in inches, centimeters, picas, points, or pixels. To change the unit of measure, click Options on the Tools menu, and then on the General tab of the Options dialog box, select the unit type you want in the Measurement Units list.

11. Double-click the text box frame to open the **Format Text Box** dialog box.

**Format Text Box**

Colors and Lines | Size | Layout | Picture | Text Box | Web

**Fill**

Color: No Fill

Transparency: 0 %

**Line**

Color: No Line

Dashed:

Style:

Weight: 0.75 pt

BorderArt...

☑ Draw border inside frame

**Preview**

**Presets**

Under Preview, select the borders you want to change, and then select the color and line styles you want.

☐ Apply settings to new text boxes

OK | Cancel | Help

**12.** On the **Colors and Lines** tab, under **Fill**, click the **Color** arrow, and in the default color palette, click the orange square (**Accent 3**). Then click **OK**.

**See Also** For information about applying a different color scheme and using custom colors, see "Creating Folded Cards" in Chapter 3, "Creating Colorful Cards and Calendars."

**13.** On the **Edit** menu, click **Select All** to select all the text in the text box.

> **Tip** You can also select all the content in a box by pressing Ctrl+A.

**14.** On the **Formatting** toolbar, click the **Font** arrow, and then in the list, click **Verdana**.

**See Also** For information about using font schemes, see "Choosing a Font Scheme" in Chapter 4, "Marketing Your Product, Service, or Organization" and "Solving Organization Problems" in Chapter 5, "Creating Text-Based Publications."

Increase Font Size

**15.** On the **Formatting** toolbar, click the **Increase Font Size** button twice, to increase the font size to 12 points.

If the font is too big, you can click the Decrease Font Size button. You can select a specific point size by clicking the Font Size arrow and clicking the size in the list.

Font Color

16. On the **Formatting** toolbar, click the **Font Color** arrow, and in the default color palette, click the white square (**Accent 5**). Then click anywhere in the text box to release the selection.

> **Tip**  To apply the color currently shown on the Font Color button, simply click the button (not its arrow).

17. Drag the bottom handle of the text box frame upward, releasing the mouse button when the dimensions shown on the status bar are **5.000 x 1.500 in**.

> **Troubleshooting**  If the dimensions don't change but the coordinates do, you missed the handle and moved the text box by dragging its frame instead of the handle. On the Standard toolbar, click the Undo button, and then try dragging the handle again.

18. Select the heading **What Is Fourth Coffee?** by dragging across or double-clicking it, and then click the **Increase Font Size** button five times to increase the font size to 22 points.

19. With the heading still selected, on the **Format** menu, click **Font** to open the **Font** dialog box.

The Sample box shows the formatting applied to the selection. As you make changes to the settings in the dialog box, the sample changes to show how the selection will look if you click Apply or OK. (Clicking Apply implements the current settings without closing the dialog box.)

**20.** Click the **Font style** arrow, and in the list, click **Bold**. Then under **Effects**, select the **Small caps** check box, and click **OK**.

You can click buttons on the formatting toolbar to change the font style of text, but to apply font effects, you have to use the Font dialog box. If you want to apply several attributes to the same text, it is often quicker to open the dialog box and apply them all from there.

**21.** On the **Format** menu, click **Character Spacing** to open the **Character Spacing** dialog box.

**22.** Under **Tracking**, click the arrow of the left box, and in the list, click **Very Loose**. Then click **OK**.

> **Tip** To copy the formatting of one word or phrase to another, select the text whose formatting you want to copy, click the Format Painter button on the Standard toolbar, and then select the text onto which you want to "paint" the formatting.

**23.** Click outside the text box to release the selection and see the results.

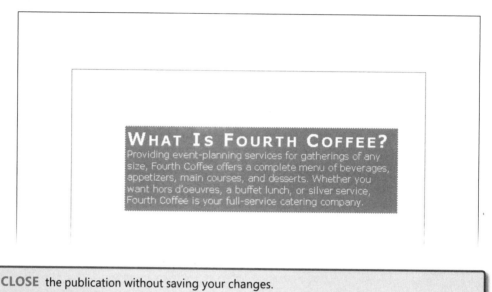

CLOSE the publication without saving your changes.

# Working with WordArt

If you want to add a fancy title to a publication, and you can't achieve the effect you want with regular text formatting, you can use *WordArt*. With WordArt, you can visually enhance text in ways that go far beyond changing a font or font effect, simply by choosing a style from a set of small *thumbnail* images arranged in a *gallery*.

> **Tip** For the best results, use WordArt to emphasize short phrases, such as *Customer Service*, or a single word, such as *Welcome*. Overusing WordArt can clutter your publication and draw attention away from your message.

You add stylized text to a publication by clicking the WordArt button on the Objects toolbar. You then select a style from the WordArt gallery, enter your text, and apply any additional formatting. Publisher inserts the text in your publication as a WordArt object that you can size and move like any other object. You can also change the shape of the object to stretch and form the letters of the text in various ways.

In this exercise, you will add a WordArt object to a publication and then modify the appearance of the text. There is no practice file for this exercise.

OPEN a blank publication, and then close the Format Publication task pane.

Insert WordArt

**1.** On the **Objects** toolbar, click the **Insert WordArt** button.

The WordArt Gallery opens, displaying the available styles.

**2.** Click the first thumbnail in the third row (the orange and yellow sample), and then click **OK**.

The Edit WordArt Text dialog box opens so that you can enter the text you want to depict as WordArt.

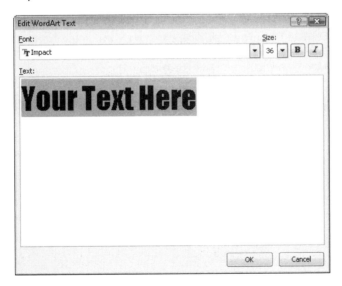

**3.** With the placeholder text selected, type Fourth Coffee, and then click **OK**.

The formatted text appears as an object in the center of the page, and Publisher displays the WordArt toolbar.

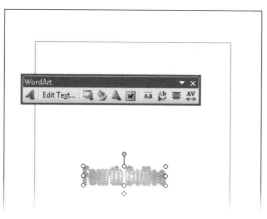

> **Tip** You can display the name of each button on the WordArt toolbar by pointing to it. The button names will give you some idea of the formatting you can apply to a WordArt object to get the effect you want.

**4.** If necessary, move the toolbar out of the way. Then move and resize the WordArt object until it spans the top of the page and is about 2 inches high.

> **Tip** Notice that the pointer position is always shown on the horizontal and vertical rulers. When dragging an object's sizing handle, you can use the insertion point position to align the sizing handle with the ruler units.

WordArt Shape

**5.** On the **WordArt** toolbar, click the **WordArt Shape** button, and then in the gallery, click the third thumbnail in the first row (**Triangle Up**).

> **Troubleshooting** If you click outside the WordArt object, it is no longer active, and the WordArt toolbar disappears. Click the WordArt object once to reactivate it and display the toolbar.

Format WordArt

**6.** On the **WordArt** toolbar, click the **Format WordArt** button.

The Format WordArt dialog box opens. This dialog box resembles the Format Text Box dialog box shown earlier in this chapter.

7. Under **Fill** on the **Colors and Lines** tab, click the **Color** arrow, and then click **Fill Effects**.

The Fill Effects dialog box opens.

8. With **Two colors** selected under **Colors** on the **Gradient** tab, click the **Color 1** arrow, and in the default palette, click the **Purple** box. Then in the **Color 2** list, click the **Gray** box.

9. Under **Shading styles**, click **Horizontal**, and under **Variants**, click the lower-left option. Then click **OK** twice.

10. Drag the yellow diamond handle to the left of the frame up until the dotted outline of the letters is aligned with about the half-inch mark on the vertical ruler.

> **Tip** The handle moves only after you release the mouse button, not while you drag it.

The letters at the sides of the WordArt object stretch so that the triangle effect is less exaggerated.

**11.** Click away from the object to release the selection and see the results.

**CLOSE** the publication without saving your changes.

# Working with Graphics

Publisher 2007 provides access to hundreds of professionally designed pieces of *clip art*—license-free graphics that often take the form of cartoons, sketches, or symbolic images, but can also include photographs, audio and video clips, and more sophisticated artwork. In a publication, you can use clip art to illustrate a point you are making or as eye-pleasing accompaniments to text. For example, you might insert an icon of an envelope to draw attention to an e-mail address, or a picture of mountains to set a "back to nature" tone.

To search for a clip art image, you display the Clip Art task pane and enter a keyword. You can search a specific Microsoft Clip Organizer collection, search for specific media types, such as photographs, and search for images on the Microsoft Office Online Web site.

**See Also**  For information about creating collections of images, see the sidebar titled "Clip Organizer," later in this chapter.

You can add illustrations created and saved in other programs or scanned photographs and illustrations to your publications. We refer to these types of graphics as *pictures*. Like clip art, pictures can be used to make your publications more attractive and visually interesting. However, pictures can also convey information in a way that words cannot. For example, you might display photographs of your company's products in a catalog or brochure.

## Graphic Formats

You can use a variety of graphic file formats in Publisher publications. Here are some of the more common formats:

- **BMP (bitmap).** Stores graphics as a series of dots, or pixels. The different types of BMP reflect the number of bits per pixel needed to store information about the graphic—the greater the number of colors, the greater the number of bits needed.

- **GIF (Graphics Interchange Format).** Common for images that appear on Web pages because they can be compressed with no loss of information and groups of them can be animated. GIFs work well for line drawings, pictures with blocks of solid color, and pictures with sharp boundaries between colors. GIFs store at most 8 bits per pixel, so they are limited to 256 colors.

- **JPEG (Joint Photographic Experts Group).** A compressed format that works well for complex graphics such as scanned photographs. Some information is lost in the compression process, but often the loss is imperceptible to the human eye. Color JPEG images store 24 bits per pixel, so they are capable of displaying more than 16 million colors. Grayscale JPEG images store 8 bits per pixel.

- **PNG (Portable Network Graphic).** Has the advantages of the GIF format but can store colors with 8, 24, or 48 bits per pixel and grayscales with 1, 2, 4, 8, or 16 bits per pixel. A PNG file can also specify whether each pixel blends with its background color and can contain color correction information so that images look accurate on a broad range of display devices. Graphics saved in this format are smaller, so the size of the publication file is also smaller.

- **TIFF (Tag Image File Format).** Stores compressed images with a flexible number of bits per pixel. Using tags, a single multi-page TIFF file can store several images, along with related information such as type of compression, orientation, and so on.

- **WMF (Windows Metafile).** A 16-bit vector graphic format commonly used in the 1990s but largely eclipsed by more modern formats suited to both print and Web applications.

## Clip Organizer

To make clip art images and other media available no matter where they are actually stored, you can catalog them in the *Microsoft Clip Organizer*. With this useful tool, you can arrange clip art images, pictures, audio clips, and video clips that are stored in different locations. You can organize media installed with Microsoft Office programs, downloaded from the Web, or obtained from other sources into existing or new collections. You can access these collections from within any Microsoft Office program.

To add an image to the Clip Organizer:

1. At the bottom of the **Clip Art** task pane, click the **Organize clips** link.

   The Favorites - Microsoft Clip Organizer window opens.

2. In the **Collection List** pane, under **My Collections**, click the **Favorites** folder.

3. On the window's **File** menu, point to **Add Clips to Organizer**, and then click **On My Own**.

   The Favorites - Add Clips To Organizer dialog box opens.

4. Navigate to and select the file you want to add to the Favorites collection, and then click the **Add** button.

   To place images in a collection other than the currently selected one, click the Add To button, and then in the Import To Collection dialog box, select or create the collection you want.

To add keywords to an image:

1. In the **Favorites – Microsoft Clip Organizer** window, point to the image, click the arrow that appears, and then click **Edit Keywords**.

   The Keywords dialog box opens.

2. In the **Keyword** box, type the word or words that you want to associate with this file (separating words and phrases with commas), and then click **Add**.

   Your keywords are added to the Keywords For Current Clip list, which already contains any previously associated keywords.

3. Click **OK** to close the **Keywords** dialog box.

To delete a clip art image from the Clip Organizer, in the Microsoft Clip Organizer window, point to the image, click the arrow that appears, click Delete From Clip Organizer, and then click OK to confirm the deletion.

## Positioning and Sizing a Graphic

After you insert a graphic into a publication, you can move and size it just as you can any other object. You can also do the following:

- *Rotate* the graphic to any angle.
- *Crop* away the parts of the graphic that you don't want to show in the publication. (The graphic itself is not altered—parts of it are simply not shown.)
- *Compress* the image to minimize the file size.

> **Tip** The file size of a publication that contains graphics can become quite large. You can shrink the size of a graphic file (without affecting the displayed graphic) by using the Compress Pictures feature. Depending on the resolution setting, you might lose some visual quality when you compress a picture. You choose the resolution you want for the pictures based on where or how the presentation will be viewed—for example, on the Web or printed. You can also set other options, such as deleting cropped areas of a picture, to achieve the best balance between quality and file size. This is especially important when you intend to distribute a publication electronically, because the file size affects how long it takes to transmit or download.

## Modifying the Appearance of a Graphic

When a graphic object is selected, Publisher displays the Picture toolbar. You can use the buttons on this toolbar to modify the appearance of the selected graphic in various ways, including the following:

- Change the color.
- Change to shades of gray (called *grayscale*), black and white, or muted shades of its original colors (called *washout*).
- Adjust the contrast.
- Adjust the brightness.
- Change the color and style of the border.
- Make parts of the graphic transparent.

And if you decide you don't like the changes you have made to a graphic, you can restore the original settings by clicking the Reset Picture button.

In this exercise, you will insert and modify a clip art image, and then insert and crop a picture. Then you will decrease the file sizes of the two graphics by compressing them.

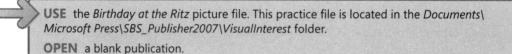

USE the *Birthday at the Ritz* picture file. This practice file is located in the *Documents\ Microsoft Press\SBS_Publisher2007\VisualInterest* folder.

OPEN a blank publication.

Picture Frame

1. On the **Objects** toolbar, click the **Picture Frame** button, and then click **Clip Art**.

> **Tip** If you are designing the layout of a publication and know you will want to insert some sort of graphic later, you can click Empty Picture Frame to insert a graphic placeholder.

The Clip Art task pane opens.

2. In the **Search for** box at the top of the task pane, type birthday. Click the **Search in** arrow, and select the **Everywhere** check box. Then click **Go**.

Thumbnails of clip art, photographs, movies, and sounds with the keyword *birthday* appear in the task pane.

> **Troubleshooting** Images sourced from Microsoft Office Online are indicated by an Internet icon in the lower-left corner of the image thumbnail. If you do not have an active Internet connection, you might not see all the clip art images shown here. In that case, pick any clip art image to follow the steps in this exercise.

**3.** Scroll the thumbnail list box, and point to any stylized drawing of a cake with candles.

A ScreenTip displays the beginning of the list of keywords associated with the image, its dimensions and file size, and its format.

**See Also** For information about common graphic formats, see the sidebar titled "Graphic Formats," earlier in this chapter.

**4.** Toward the bottom of the list box, click one of the one-color cake silhouettes.

Publisher inserts the image into the publication and displays the Picture toolbar.

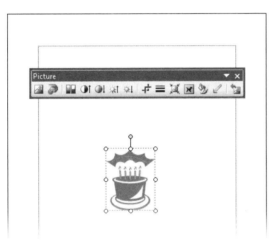

Format Picture

**5.** With the clip art image still selected, on the **Picture** toolbar, click the **Format Picture** button.

The Format Picture dialog box opens.

> **Important**  The following formatting choices apply to the cake image we selected. If you selected a different image, you might want to choose different formatting options.

6. Under **Image control** on the **Picture** tab, click the **Recolor** button.

> **Troubleshooting**  If you chose a more-complex graphic than the one shown in the example, you might not be able to recolor it.

7. In the **Recolor Picture** dialog box, click the **Color** arrow, and in the default color palette, click the **Purple** box. Then click **OK**.

8. In the **Format Picture** dialog box, change the **Brightness** setting to 25% and the **Contrast** setting to 75%.

9. Click the **Colors and Lines** tab, and under **Fill**, click the **Color** arrow, and click the **Gray** box. Then under **Line**, click the **Color** arrow, and click the **Purple** box.

10. Click the **Size** tab, and under **Scale**, change the **Height** setting to 75%. Then click the **Width** box.

The Width setting changes to 75% because the aspect ratio of the graphic is locked. You can change the proportions of the image by clearing the Lock Aspect Ratio check box.

**11.** Click the **Layout** tab, and under **Position on page**, change the **Horizontal** setting to 1″ and the **Vertical** setting to 1″. Then click **OK**.

The small graphic jumps to the upper-left corner of the page, displaying its new purple and gray color scheme. (If necessary, move the toolbar to see the image.)

**12.** Click a blank area of the page to release the selection, and then close the **Clip Art** task pane.

**13.** On the **Objects** toolbar, click the **Picture Frame** button, and then click **Picture from File**.

> **Troubleshooting** If you don't release the selection before clicking the button, the new picture will replace the clip art image.

**14.** Move the pointer over the page below the clip art image, and drag to create a frame about 4 inches square. (Use the rulers or the size indicator on the status bar to guide you.)

When you release the mouse button, Publisher displays the Insert Picture dialog box.

**See Also** For information about how to move around in dialog boxes such as this one, see "Saving and Closing Publications" in Chapter 1, "Getting Started with Publisher 2007."

**15.** If the contents of the *VisualInterest* folder are not displayed, navigate to the *Documents\Microsoft Press\SBS_Publisher2007\VisualInterest* folder, and double-click the **Birthday at the Ritz** picture.

Publisher inserts the picture in the frame you drew on the page and displays the Picture toolbar.

**16.** If necessary, move the Picture toolbar out of the way. Then drag the lower-right handle of the frame down and to the right until the picture fills the width of the page.

Crop

**17.** With the picture still selected, on the **Picture** toolbar, click the **Crop** button.

Cropping handles appear in the corners and on the sides of the picture.

Cropping handles

**18.** Drag the top cropping handle down to the top of the candle flames. Then drag the left and right cropping handles to tightly focus the picture on the plate and the little cake.

**19.** Click the **Crop** button to hide the cropping handles.

Line/Border Style

**20.** With the picture still selected, on the **Picture** toolbar, click the **Line/Border Style** button, and in the list, click the **3 pt** line. Then click a blank area of the page to see the results.

Compress
Pictures

**21.** Click the picture, and then on the **Picture** toolbar, click the **Compress Pictures** button.

The Compress Pictures dialog box opens.

Notice the current size of the image files and the estimated size after compression using the default settings. Unless you select the Apply To Selected Pictures Only check box, Publisher will compress all the pictures in the publication, not only the selected picture.

22. Under **Compression options,** leave all the check boxes selected. Under **Target Output**, click **Web**.

Notice that the estimated size after compression using the new settings is much smaller. The resolution for displaying graphics on the Web is much lower than the resolution for printing.

23. Click **Compress**. Then click **Yes** to apply picture optimization.

Publisher compresses the pictures and deletes the cropped parts of the picture. If you were to save the file now, the compressed pictures would result in a smaller file size.

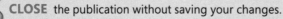

**CLOSE** the publication without saving your changes.

# Working with Shapes

Publisher provides tools for creating several types of shapes, including lines, arrows, ovals, rectangles, stars, banners, and many more. With a little imagination, you will discover countless ways to create drawings by combining shapes.

To create a shape in Publisher, you click a shape button on the Objects toolbar and then drag the crosshair pointer across the page to define the size of the shape. After you draw the shape, it is surrounded by a set of handles, indicating that it is selected. (You can select a shape at any time by simply clicking it.)

> **Tip** To draw a circle or square, click the Oval or Rectangle shape, and hold down the Shift key while you drag.

You can easily add text to a shape. Simply select the shape by clicking it, and start typing. You can then format the text by clicking buttons on the Formatting toolbar or by making selections in the Font dialog box.

## Manipulating a Shape

To move a shape from one location to another on the same page, you simply point to the shape, and when the pointer becomes a four-headed arrow, drag the shape to its new location, using the coordinates shown on the status bar to position it precisely. (You can create a copy of a selected shape by dragging it while holding down the Ctrl key.) You can also reposition a shape by changing settings on the Layout tab of the Format AutoShape dialog box.

> **Tip** If you hold down the Shift key while moving a shape, you can move it only horizontally or vertically in a straight line.

The handles around a selected shape serve the same sizing and rotating purposes as those around any other object. You can use the dimensions shown on the status bar to adjust the size precisely, or you can set the size of the shape on the Size tab of the Format AutoShape dialog box. You can rotate it by using the Rotate Or Flip command on the Arrange menu.

After drawing a shape, you can fill it with color by using the settings on the Colors And Lines tab of the Format AutoShape dialog box or by selecting a color from the palette displayed when you click the Fill Color arrow on the Formatting toolbar. You can change the color and width of the border on the Color And Lines tab of the Format AutoShape dialog box, or change only its width by clicking the Line/Border Style button on the Formatting toolbar.

> **Tip** Having made changes to one shape, you can easily apply the same attributes to another shape by clicking the shape that has the desired attributes, clicking the Format Painter button on the Standard toolbar, and then clicking the shape to which you want to copy the attributes.
>
> If you want to apply the attributes of a shape to all future shapes in the same publication (for example, if you want all shapes to be red), double-click the shape, and on the Colors And Lines tab of the Format AutoShape dialog box, select the Apply Settings To New AutoShapes check box.

## Connecting and Grouping Shapes

To show a relationship between two shapes, you can connect them with a line by joining special handles called *connection points*. Moving a connected shape also moves the line, maintaining the relationship between the connected shapes.

When you create a drawing composed of multiple shapes, you can *group* them so that you can edit, copy, and move them as a unit. You can select an individual shape within the group and change its attributes—for example, its color or the weight of its border. You can *ungroup* the grouped shapes at any time and *regroup* them after making changes.

In this exercise, you will draw several shapes of the same color. Then you will connect two shapes and format the connection line. Finally, you will group and ungroup the shapes. There is no practice file for this exercise.

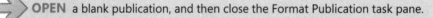

**OPEN** a blank publication, and then close the Format Publication task pane.

AutoShapes

1. On the **Objects** toolbar, click the **AutoShapes** button, point to **Basic Shapes**, and then click the third shape in the second row (**Isosceles Triangle**).

2. Move the pointer over the page, and starting about 1 inch below the top margin guide, drag to draw a triangle about 1 inch tall and 1/2 inch wide.

3. On the **Arrange** menu, point to **Rotate or Flip**, and then click **Flip Vertical**.

   The triangle is now upside down.

4. Double-click the shape, and on the **Colors and Lines** tab of the **Format AutoShape** dialog box, change the **Color** setting under **Fill** to **Orange**. Then select the **Apply settings to new AutoShapes** check box, and click **OK**.

5. On the **Objects** toolbar, click the **Oval** button, hold down the ⇧ Shift key, and drag a circle above the triangle with a diameter slightly smaller than the triangle's side.

Oval

   When you release the mouse button, Publisher fills the circle with the orange color you specified for all shapes in this publication.

> **Tip** If you click a shape button on the Objects toolbar and then change your mind about drawing the shape, you can release the shape by pressing the Esc key.

6. On the **Objects** toolbar, click the **Oval** button, and drag an oval about 1.5 inches wide to the right of the circle.

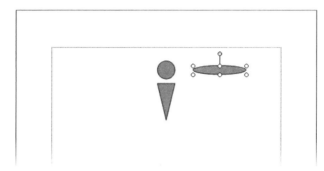

7. On the **Objects** toolbar, click the **AutoShapes** button, point to **Connectors**, and then click the first shape in the third row (**Curved Connector**).

8. Point to the triangle, and when blue handles appear, drag a line from the upper-right handle of the triangle to the bottom handle of the oval.

   Publisher joins the two shapes with a curved connecting line. Red handles appear at each end of the line, indicating that the shapes are connected. A yellow diamond-shaped handle in the center of the line provides a means to adjust the curve of the line.

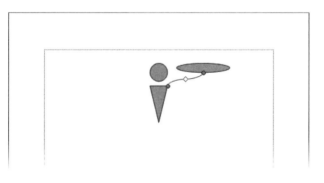

> **Troubleshooting** The yellow handle appears only if the line is long enough to support it. If you do not see the yellow handle, drag the oval slightly up or to the right to lengthen the connector line.

9. Double-click the line (not its handle), and under **Line** on the **Colors and Lines** tab of the **Format AutoShape** dialog box, change the **Color** to **Orange** and the **Weight** to **6 pt**. Then click **OK**.

**10.** Click the oval, and move it to the left, close to the circle.

Publisher adjusts the length and curve of the connecting line.

**11.** Click the line, and drag the yellow diamond handle down to create a smooth curve. Then click a blank area of the page to see the results.

**12.** Select the four shapes by holding down the ⌈ Shift ⌋ key as you click each one in turn.

Notice that each shape has its own set of handles.

**13.** On the **Arrange** menu, click **Group**.

Publisher groups the shapes together with only one set of handles around the edge of the entire group. When the group is selected, the Ungroup Objects button appears below it so that you can ungroup the shapes at any time.

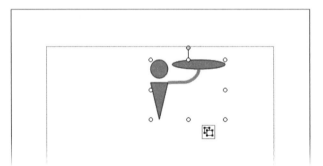

**14.** Point to any shape in the group, and when the pointer changes to a four-headed arrow, drag the grouped object to the upper-left corner of the page until the co-ordinates are **1.000, 1.000 in**.

The entire group moves.

**15.** Click away from the individual shape to release the selection, and then click the grouped shape to select it. Point to the lower-right handle and drag up and to the left until the dimensions of the grouped object are **1.500 x 1.000 in**.

**16.** Click a blank area of the page to see the results.

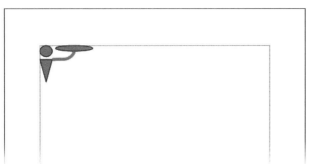

Ungroup Objects

**17.** Click the grouped shape to select it, and then click the **Ungroup Objects** button.

Publisher ungroups the object into individual shapes, which are all selected, and displays the Group Objects button. You can now adjust the size and position of individual shapes.

Group Objects

**18.** Click the **Group Objects** button.

Publisher regroups the shapes. Now suppose you want to add a shape to the group.

**19.** On the **Objects** toolbar, click the **AutoShape** button, point to **Basic Shapes**, and then click the third shape in the first row (**Trapezoid**).

**20.** Draw a tiny "cup" on top of the oval "tray," hold down the [ Shift ] key, click any of the other shapes, and then click the **Group** button.

Publisher adds the cup shape to the group.

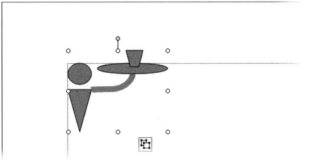

CLOSE the publication without saving your changes.

# Working with Pre-Designed Visual Elements

Publisher excels at helping you create visually exciting publications. One of the ways it provides assistance is by offering hundreds of ready-made visual elements that you can insert in a publication with a couple of clicks.

To simplify the use of these visual elements, Publisher 2007 organizes them in categories in the Design Gallery. Many of the elements have a common design and color scheme to give your publications a consistent look. When you are more familiar with color schemes and themes, you will be able to customize the colors of these elements, but for now, we will show you how to use the default Design Gallery elements to add professional touches to your publications.

**See Also**  For information about applying a different color scheme and using custom colors, see "Creating Folded Cards" in Chapter 3, "Creating Colorful Cards and Calendars."

You cannot add a customized element to the Design Gallery, even if you originally inserted it in your publication from that gallery. If you want to reuse a customized Design Gallery element, or any other object, you can copy and paste it between publications or you can add it to the Content Library.

**See Also**  For information about storing objects for use in other publications, see "Adding Items to the Content Library" in Chapter 4, "Marketing Your Product, Service, or Organization."

In this exercise, you will insert ready-made elements from three categories of the Design Gallery into a publication. There is no practice file for this exercise.

> **OPEN** a blank publication, and then close the Format Publication task pane.

Design Gallery
Object

1. On the **Objects** toolbar, click the **Design Gallery Object** button.

   The Design Gallery opens. The left pane displays a list of categories. Clicking a category in the left pane displays the available Design Gallery objects in the right pane.

   Notice that the objects available in the Accent Box category are all depicted in the same color scheme.

**2.** In the left pane, click **Borders**. Then in the right pane, double-click **Stacked Corners**.

Publisher inserts an asymmetrical border around the perimeter of the page.

**3.** With the border selected, press the ➡ key and the ⬇ key repeatedly until the blue margin guides are approximately centered within the border.

The border consists of sets of overlapping rectangles. You can move the entire border because all of its components are grouped to form one object that can be treated as a single unit.

**See Also**   For information about grouping objects, see "Connecting and Grouping Shapes," earlier in this chapter.

4. Display the **Design Gallery** again, click **Dots** in the left pane, and then double-click **Diamond** in the right pane.

5. With the row of dots selected, point to one of the corner handles on the left, and drag until the row of diamonds extends to the blue margin guide on the left. Then repeat this step to extend the row to the blue margin guide on the right.

6. Display the **Design Gallery**, and in the left pane, click **Coupons**.

   The Design Gallery displays the three available coupon designs, along with options for customizing them.

7. In the middle pane, click **Top Oval**. In the **Options** pane, under **Border**, click **Basic dots**. Then click **Insert Object**.

8. Drag the coupon to the area below the row of diamonds. Then use the corner handles to enlarge the coupon until it fills the available space.

   By inserting the three ready-made objects from the Design Gallery, you have created this basic flyer:

You can customize the color and appearance of the placeholder text and graphic elements as you want.

**CLOSE** the publication without saving your changes, and if you are not continuing directly on to the next chapter, quit Publisher.

## Key Points

- Creating and manipulating visual elements is a basic Publisher skill that you will use when working in most publications.

- You can reposition most elements by dragging them, and you can resize elements by dragging their sizing handles.

- You can group elements together to manipulate them as a single unit.

- Before you spend time creating graphics, check for publicly available clip art and ready-made Design Gallery elements.

# Chapter at a Glance

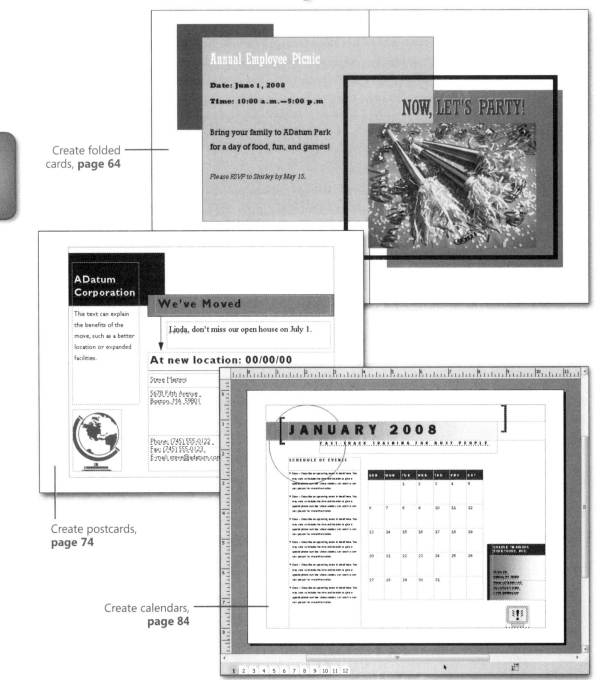

Create folded cards, **page 64**

Create postcards, **page 74**

Create calendars, **page 84**

# 3 Creating Colorful Cards and Calendars

---

**In this chapter, you will learn to:**

✔ Create folded cards.

✔ Create postcards.

✔ Create calendars.

✔ Package publications for printing.

---

Cards and calendars can be among the easiest publications to produce. Microsoft Office Publisher 2007 provides dozens of attractive templates from which you can create and personalize these items, perhaps to send to friends or clients. However, if you intend to distribute a lot of them, you might need to do some advance planning. Several of the decisions you need to make before creating cards and calendars for large-scale distribution revolve around the cost, in time and money, of printing the final product.

In this chapter, we discuss issues such as layout, color, paper, printing, and mailing, while showing you how to produce a folded card, a postcard, and three types of calendars. You also learn how to save time when creating a multi-page publication by applying formatting to the underlying master page.

**See Also** Do you need only a quick refresher on the topics in this chapter? See the Quick Reference entries on pages xxvii–xli.

**Important** Before you can use the practice files in this chapter, you need to install them from the book's companion CD to their default location. See "Using the Book's CD" on page xvii for more information.

**Troubleshooting** Graphics and operating system–related instructions in this book reflect the Windows Vista user interface. If your computer is running Windows XP and you experience trouble following the instructions as written, please refer to the "Information for Readers Running Windows XP" section at the beginning of this book.

# Creating Folded Cards

The cards that you buy in a store are usually folded publications with text and graphic elements on all sides. You can print cards that you create in Publisher on both sides of the paper, or you can simulate this effect by printing the content on one side of the paper and then folding it in four. Microsoft Office Publisher 2007 comes with many templates for two types of folded cards: Greeting Cards and Invitation Cards. In addition, five tent-fold templates are available in the Postcards category.

## Choosing a Design or Layout

When you choose certain publication types, including Greeting Cards or Invitation Cards, in the Getting Started window, the thumbnails for two kinds of templates appear in the center pane:

- **Design templates.** Templates such as the Thank You type of greeting card or the Party type of invitation card are based on one of the classic Publisher designs, such as Accent Box, Capsules, or Quadrant. When you click one of these templates, the Page Size and Layout settings under Options in the right pane are unavailable, so you cannot change the design.

- **Layout templates.** Templates such as the Birth Announcement type of greeting card or the Birthday Party type of invitation card are based on a layout, such as Frames, Portal, or Radius. When you click one of these templates, the Page Size and Layout settings under Options in the right pane are available, so you can change them.

The Page Size option determines whether your publication will occupy a quarter page or a half page, with the crease on the top or on the side. The Layout option determines which page layout will be applied to the card. You can change the page size and customize the layout after you have created the card, but with so many options to choose from, you can save time by choosing the template that is closest to the effect you want.

If you click a layout template and then change the Page Size option, most of the layout thumbnails in the center pane change to reflect the size you selected. If you change the Layout option, most of the thumbnails change to reflect the layout you selected. In this way, you can get a good idea of the range of possibilities. (A few layout templates are fixed and don't change when you select a different option.)

> **Tip** Each time you open a new instance of the Getting Started window, it displays the template thumbnails with the default settings. You can experiment with changes to the color scheme, font scheme, page size, and layout until you find the combination you want.

Every publication, even a blank one, has a color scheme, a font scheme, and a set of information associated with it. You can change these options after you create a publication, but you can save time by specifying all three at the time of creation.

## Changing the Color Scheme

A *color scheme* consists of eight complementary colors designed to be used for the following elements of a publication:

- The Main color is for the text.
- The Accent 1 through Accent 5 colors are for objects other than text.
- The Hyperlink color is for indicating hyperlinks that have not been clicked.
- The Followed Hyperlink color is for indicating visited hyperlinks.

Understanding color schemes can help you create professional-looking publications that use an appropriate balance of color. You are not limited to using the colors in a publication's color scheme, nor are you limited to using the color schemes that come with Publisher, but because they have been selected by professional designers based on good design principles, using them ensures that your publications will be more pleasing to the eye.

The Color Scheme list in the Customize pane that appears when you select a publication type displays four of the eight colors in each scheme—Accent 1 through Accent 4—to give you an idea of the feeling evoked by that combination of colors. (By default, the Main text color is always black.) When you find the color scheme you want, clicking it changes the color scheme not only of the selected thumbnail but of all the thumbnails in the center pane.

After you create a publication, you can switch to a different color scheme by clicking Color Schemes in the Format Publication task pane. (If the task pane is closed, you can click Color Schemes on the Format menu to open it with the color scheme list displayed.)

> **Tip** If none of the color schemes is exactly what you are looking for, you can create your own by selecting a starting color scheme (preferably one that is close to what you want), clicking Create New Color Scheme at the bottom of the Color Schemes pane, and then choosing colors in the Create New Color Scheme dialog box. After you save the scheme with a name of your choosing, it appears at the top of the Color Schemes list both in the Format Publication task pane and in the Getting Started window, and you can apply it to any publication in the usual way.

**See Also** For information about font schemes, see "Choosing a Font Scheme" in Chapter 4, "Marketing Your Product, Service, or Organization."

## Ink and Paper

It's fun to play around with the Publisher color schemes to determine the precise combination of colors that meets the needs of your publication and your goals. However, bear in mind that, whether you use cartridge ink to print copies of an invitation on your own printer or print copies at a commercial copy or print shop, color costs money.

For small print jobs—for example, 10 invitations—you will probably want to buy a package of high-quality paper and print the copies yourself. But for larger print jobs—for example, 100 invitations—you might be tempted to use the high-speed color copier at your local copy shop. How much will those 100 copies cost you? It depends on a lot of different options: the quality, color, and weight (usually expressed in pounds per 1000 sheets) of the paper, the number of ink colors, the dimensions of the publication, whether it requires folding, and so on. The price typically ranges from $0.75 per copy to more than $1.25 per copy. Depending on the purpose of the publication, that might be way too expensive.

A quick way of getting an idea of the cost of your project is to upload your publication to an online printer, select the options you want, and then see what the price would be. (Just be careful to not click the order button unless you're sure you want to spend the money.)

If you need many copies and can't afford new ink cartridges or commercial copies, one alternative is to make creative use of the color black. Black ink on plain white paper typically costs $0.08 a copy at a copy or print shop (but you can often find cheaper deals). Black ink on colored paper, higher-quality paper, or fancy preprinted paper is more expensive, but is certainly more affordable than color copies. Some copy shops even have promotions where, on specific days, paper of a specific color is the same price as white paper.

When using colored or patterned paper as part of the design of a publication, you will obviously need to use common sense to ensure that your publication is attractive and readable. But if cost is a concern, this option might provide a way of introducing color into a publication without breaking the budget.

## Color Models

On the Standard tab of the Colors dialog box, you can select from 127 colors presented in a honeycomb spectrum and a 15-shade grayscale.

On the Custom tab of the Colors dialog box, you can select from the following three color models and then specify a color either visually by dragging a crosshair across a spectrum or by entering values in boxes:

- *RGB*. This model is a method of creating colors by using combinations of red, green, and blue. The model is linked to the development of the cathode ray tube (CRT), which was for many years the standard technology used in televisions and computer monitors.

- *HSL*. This model analyzes a color in terms of its position in the rainbow (hue), its purity or vividness (saturation), and its brightness (luminance). Essentially, saturation is a measure of the amount of white added to the hue, and luminance is the measure of the amount of black added to the hue.

- *CMYK*. This model is a method of creating colors by using combinations of cyan (bluish-green), magenta (purplish-red), yellow, and black. Before the advent of digital printing, almost all colored printing involved a printing process that uses four plates to print the four CMYK colors in such a way that they are perceived as other colors. Because this color model is closely tied to this printing process, cyan, magenta, yellow, and black are also known as *process colors*.

On the PANTONE tab of the dialog box, you can specify a color from the *Pantone Matching System (PMS)*. This proprietary system was developed by Pantone, Inc. to give designers in color-critical industries such as publishing, packaging, decorating, and architecture the means to communicate with printers and manufacturers. This system uses sheets of numbered color swatches to identify colors created with precise amounts of pigment. For example, the purple color used in official materials produced by our company, OTSI, is PMS 520 C. (The C stands for *Coated*, meaning the color that results when PMS 520 is used on coated, or shiny, paper.) Because Pantone colors are premixed to a single ink or dye, they are sometimes referred to as *spot colors*.

As a general rule, you can use the RGB or HSL color model for publications designed to be viewed on the computer screen or digitally printed. Use the CMYK or Pantone color model for publications that will be commercially printed in large quantities or that require specific color matching.

## Using Non-Color-Scheme Colors

Although working with the eight colors of a harmonious color scheme simplifies the process of designing a publication, you might want to use a larger palette of colors. You can add colors that are not part of the color scheme by selecting the element whose color you want to change and then choosing from the almost infinite spectrum of colors available from the Colors dialog box.

After you use a non-color-scheme color in a publication, it becomes available on all the palettes that appear when you click buttons that apply color—for example, the Font Color button on the Formatting toolbar. The color remains on the palettes associated with the publication—even if you stop using the color or change the color scheme applied to the publication.

## Choosing Text

Most publications that you create based on Publisher templates will include placeholders for text. The placeholder text might be suggested wording or simply indicate the type of information to insert in that text box. When you create an invitation, Publisher suggests text that is appropriate to the invitation template you choose. You can change the text to your own words, or choose from approximately 150 two-part verses (in 23 occasion-specific categories, including business, personal, and holiday occasions) designed to adorn the cover and interior of a folded card.

In this exercise, you will create a folded card based on a layout template. You will change the color scheme before and after you create the publication, change the verse, apply different colors, and change the stacking order of elements on the page.

**USE** the *FoldedCard* publication. This file is located in the *Documents\Microsoft Press\ SBS_Publisher2007\CardsCalendars* folder.
**BE SURE TO** start Publisher and display the Getting Started window before beginning this exercise.

1. In the **Publication Types** list, click **Invitation Cards**, and then scroll the center pane to get an idea of the range of publications available.

2. In the category list, click **Party**, and then in the **Party** category, click (don't double-click) the **Blends** thumbnail.

Notice in the right pane that the Page Size and Layout options are unavailable (gray), indicating that this is a general design template rather than a layout template.

3. In the category list, click **Theme Party**, and then in the **Theme Party** category, click the **Picnic** thumbnail.

Notice in the right pane that the Page Size and Layout options are available, indicating that this is a layout template.

4. Under **Options** in the right pane, click the **Page size** arrow, and then in the list, click **Quarter-page top fold**. Then click the **Layout** arrow, and toward the top of the list, click **Juxtaposition**.

The preview thumbnail changes as you select each option.

5. Scroll the center pane, and notice that Publisher has applied your choices to the thumbnails of all templates that do not have a fixed layout.

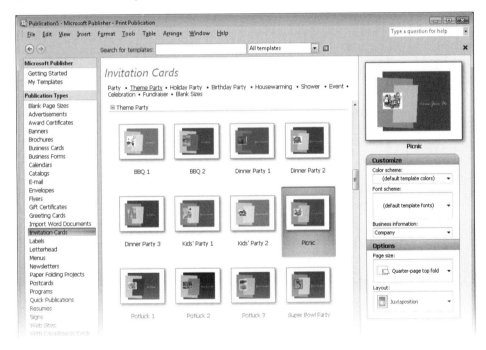

6. Under **Customize** in the right pane, click the **Color scheme** arrow, and scroll through the list, noting all the different options.

7. Toward the bottom of the list, click **Oriel**, and then scroll the center pane.

Publisher has applied the Oriel color scheme to all the templates.

**8.** In the **Party** category, double-click the **Blocks** thumbnail.

Publisher creates an invitation card divided into four pages (the front of the card, the inside spread, and the back of the card). The publication reflects the Oriel color scheme you selected, but because Blocks is a design template, the publication is a half-page side-fold card instead of the quarter-page top-fold orientation that you selected in step 4. The Format Publication task pane displays options for refining the layout and formatting of the publication.

> **Tip** Although you cannot change the orientation and size of this design template in the Getting Started window, you can change them after you create the card by clicking Change Page Size in the Format Publication task pane to display the Page Setup dialog box. Be aware however, that the layout of this design is tailored specifically to a vertical half-page card. If you change the orientation or size, you will need to manually adjust the layout to fit your selection.

If you have already saved text in an information set as we did in Chapter 1, "Getting Started with Publisher 2007," your organization name appears on page 1 above the invitation verse, and on page 4.

> **Troubleshooting** Information inserted from an information set is indicated by a blue dotted underline. The dotted underline is an on-screen indicator, and will not be printed.
>
> The information set does not automatically replace the placeholder text in templates that you download from Microsoft Office Online. To replace or update a placeholder with text or a logo saved in an information set, point to the placeholder, click the smart tag that appears, and then click Update From Business Information Set.

**See Also** For information about information sets, see "Storing Personal and Company Information" in Chapter 1, "Getting Started with Publisher 2007."

Page 2

**9.** On the page sorter, click the **Page 2** button to display pages 2 and 3.

**10.** In the **Format Publication** task pane, under **Invitation Options**, click **Select a suggested verse**.

The Suggested Verse dialog box opens.

**Suggested Verse**

Category:   General Party

Available messages:                    First message part:

Celebrate summer...
The boss invites you to din
It's a celebration...
We've worked hard.
We'd like to thank you.
It's a party in honor of...
You're invited...                      Second message part:
We're delighted to invite y
It's a special occasion.
Our company requests...
Loosen up!
We're having a hoedown.

                                       OK          Cancel

**11.** Click the **Category** arrow and scroll the list of options to see what's available. Then click **General Party**, and in the **Available messages** list, click **We've worked hard.**

Publisher displays the message text that will appear on the front page of the card in the First Message Part window, and the text that will appear inside the card in the Second Message Part window.

**12.** Click **OK** to insert the selected text.

The messages on pages 1 and 3 change to reflect your choice. You can customize the messages and the other text on the card to suit your needs. In this exercise, we will focus on adjusting the color.

**13.** Display page 4.

The current color scheme does not coordinate well with the company logo.

**14.** In the **Format Publication** task pane, click **Color Schemes**, and then click various color schemes, observing the effect on the card to the right.

Notice that the first color in each scheme (Accent 1) is always assigned to the vertical block at the right edge of the card, the second color (Accent 2) is assigned to the middle panel, and the fourth color (Accent 4) is assigned to the left panel.

**15.** In the **Apply a color scheme** list, click **Harbor**.

**16.** Display page 2, and then click **Now, let's party!**

> **Troubleshooting**  If clicking the text doesn't select it all, click in the text box and then press Ctrl+A.

Font Color

**17.** On the **Formatting** toolbar, click the **Font Color** arrow, and then click **More Colors**.

The Colors dialog box opens with the Standard color spectrum displayed.

**18.** In the **Colors** spectrum, click the dark red hexagon.

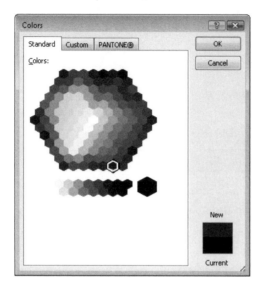

Format Painter

**19.** Click **OK**. Then with the text still selected, on the **Standard** toolbar, click the **Format Painter** button once.

> **Tip** Format Painter is a nifty tool that allows you to copy multiple formatting characteristics from one element to another. To copy formatting to only one element, click the Format Painter button once. To copy formatting to multiple elements, double-click the Format Painter button. The feature will then remain active until you either press the Esc key or click the Format Painter button again.

**20.** In the center square, click **INVITATION TITLE**.

The text changes to the same font, color, and size as the text in the right square.

Decrease
Font Size

**21.** On the **Formatting** toolbar, click the **Decrease Font Size** button three times, and then click a blank area of the publication to see the results.

**22.** In the center of the page spread, click the large square containing the invitation details once.

Publisher selects the grouped objects on the page spread.

**23.** Click the square a second time.

Publisher selects only the large square, as indicated by the gray handles.

**See Also** For information about grouped objects, see "Connecting and Grouping Shapes" in Chapter 2, "Creating Visual Interest."

Line Color

**24.** On the **Formatting** toolbar, click the **Line Color** arrow.

The dark red color you applied in step 19 from the Colors dialog box appears on the palette below the eight scheme colors.

**25.** Click the **Dark Red** square.

As you can see, the non-color-scheme color is available for use with all color formatting tools.

Fill Color

**26.** Click the bottom or right edge of the gray square on page 3 twice to select it (not the heavy black outline). Then on the **Formatting** toolbar, click the **Fill Color** arrow, and click the sixth color (**Hyperlink**) square.

> **Tip** Pointing to a color displays the purpose and the name or value of the color in a ScreenTip.

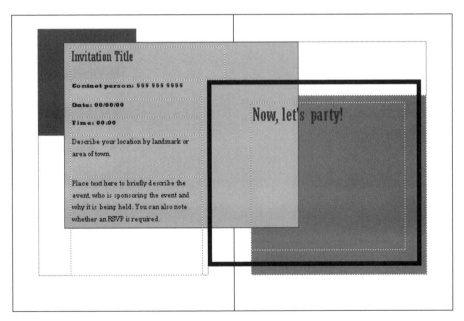

**27.** Open the *FoldedCard* practice file from the *Documents\Microsoft Press\SBS_ Publisher2007\CardsCalendars* folder to see further examples of the types of changes you can make. Use what you have learned about color to enhance the card in various ways. You might also want to use the skills you learned in Chapter 2, "Creating Visual Interest," to create eye-appeal by adding graphic elements.

**CLOSE** the open publications without saving your changes.

### Impact of Color

If you are creating publications for business purposes, bear in mind that the colors you use are just as important as the text and graphics. Different colors can send different messages. For example, "cool" colors such as green, blue, and violet are associated with water and pastoral settings and can imply peace and tranquility. On the other hand, "warm" colors such as red, orange, and yellow are associated with fire and can imply energy and intensity, or even aggression.

Be aware of these factors when selecting colors for a publication:

- Cool colors tend to recede and are ideal as background colors. Warm colors tend to advance and are good for calling attention to a specific object.

- Bright colors tend to bring objects forward visually. Muted or darker colors tend to make objects recede.

- Placing colors with the same intensity, such as red and green, next to each other can make it hard for some people to distinguish the objects.

- Color can be used to highlight information, but be careful about the implications of some colors. For example, red is commonly used for negative numbers.

- Using too many colors is distracting and creates a hodge-podge where no particular object stands out on the page.

## Creating Postcards

Using postcards is a simple way to send information to customers, club members, family, or friends. Publisher comes with many templates for two-sided postcards. Most are designed to occupy a quarter page, but a few have quarter-page or half-page options. All have a primary side called Side 1 and a secondary side called Side 2, with most of the layout options for the second side including space for an address and postage.

## Printing Both Sides of Thick Paper

Before you create a two-sided publication such as a postcard, you need to decide how you will print it. Because postcards are designed to be mailed, the paper they are printed on has to be substantial enough to withstand sorting and bagging processes without crumpling or tearing.

If you want to print only a few cards, you can buy postcard paper, also called *card stock*, at an office supply store and try printing your publication yourself. Costs vary enormously depending on the quality of the paper, its size, its color, and whether it is has a preprinted design. But at the cheap end of the scale, you can figure on about $0.12 per card.

To print on both sides of the paper, either you need a printer that supports *duplex* printing or you need to print Side 1, flip the paper over, and then print Side 2. Before you take the second route, you should run the Two-Sided Printing Setup Wizard to ensure that you correctly feed the paper; otherwise you might end up with both Side 1 and Side 2 printed on the same side of the card, or printed with different top sides. To run the wizard, click Print on the File menu, and under the Preview box in the Print dialog box, click Show How To Insert Paper. Then click Run The Two-Sided Printing Setup Wizard.

> **Important**  Depending on your printer, you might need to manually feed each sheet of card stock rather than loading up your paper tray with multiple sheets. Some printers handle card stock better than others, and just because your printer successfully prints on one side, you shouldn't assume it will successfully print both sides. Card stock that has been through a printer once might jam because of curling, or the ink from the first side might be picked up by the printer's roller and transferred as a shadow to the second side. So be sure to run tests with regular paper and then with one sheet of card stock before printing many postcards.

If you want to print many postcards and printing them yourself is not an option, you can take your publication to a copy or print shop. However, if cost is an issue, be sure to check prices first. A sheet of four double-sided postcards will cost you as much as $2.20 each on regular card stock or $2.40 each on shiny photo paper. Cutting the sheets into four is an additional cost. If you don't need the postcards within the day, you can upload your publication to an online print shop to save a bit of money.

**Online Printing Services**

Several printers who specialize in printing cards and postcards offer their services on the Web. Some of these Web sites are intuitive to use and provide cost calculators to give immediate pricing for exactly the number of postcards you need. A few options include:

- iPrint (*www.iprint.com*)
- 48HourPrint (*www.48hourprint.com*)
- PrintingForLess (*www.printingforless.com*)
- MyPrintShopOnline (*www.myprintshoponline.com*)
- FedEx Kinko's Print Online (*www.fedex.com/us/officeprint/main/*)

Online printing services can be remarkably inexpensive compared to brick-and-mortar shops. Some online vendors also offer shipping services, so you can upload your publication and an address list and leave the rest to them.

## Using Mail Merge

If you communicate with customers or members of an organization by means of postcards and other marketing pieces that are sent to everyone on a mailing list, you might want to use a process called *mail merge*. This process combines the static information in a publication with the variable information in a *data source* (a mailing list or any other type of database) to create one copy of the merged publication for every record in the data source.

The data source is a structured document, such as a Microsoft Office Word table, a Microsoft Office Excel worksheet, a Microsoft Office Access database table, or a Microsoft Office Outlook contacts list. You can use an existing data source, or you can create a new one as part of the mail merge process.

To tell Publisher what information to pull from the data source and where to put it, you insert *data fields* into the publication. These fields correspond to the field names (usually column headings) in the data source. For example, the address area of a postcard usually contains an address block consisting of fields for the name and address of each recipient. After you enter the data fields in the publication, each field is enclosed in *chevrons*—for example, «FirstName».

After you specify the data source you want to use and insert the appropriate data fields into the publication, you can either send the merged publications directly to the printer or you can merge them one after the other into a new publication, as separate pages. If you merge to a new publication, you have another chance to review and, if necessary, edit the merged copies before sending them to the printer.

This might sound like a complicated process, but Publisher makes it simple with the Mail Merge Wizard, a three-step wizard that leads you through the mail merge process from start to finish.

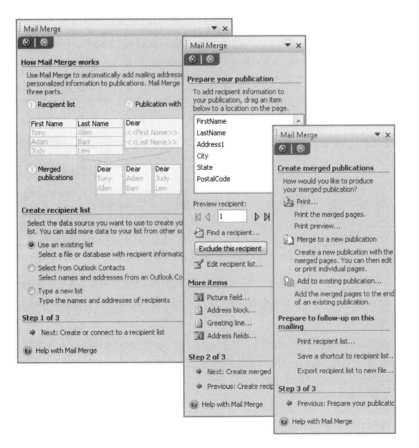

## Catalog Merge

Publisher offers several booklet-style catalog templates into which you can insert product information. If this information is stored in an Excel workbook or an Access database, you can use catalog merge to merge the product information into the catalog publication at printing time.

Catalog merge works pretty much the same way as mail merge. You can link to an existing data source or create a new one. When using an existing data source, you can filter the information or exclude specific records. This means you can tailor each printing of the catalog—for example, for a particular occasion or season.

If you frequently use catalogs as a marketing tool, it is worth taking the time to set up your product or service information in a workbook or database so that you can maintain it in one location and avoid having to retype it every time you need it. You might even consider storing information such as team or membership lists this way so that you can use Publisher and catalog merge to produce professional looking rosters.

In this exercise, you will create a postcard, insert data fields based on an existing data source, and then perform a mail merge operation to create copies with preprinted names and addresses, ready for mailing.

**USE** the *DataSource* workbook. This practice file is located in the *Documents\Microsoft Press\SBS_Publisher2007\CardsCalendars* folder.
**BE SURE TO** display the Getting Started window before beginning this exercise.

1. In the **Publication Types** list, click **Postcards**, and scroll the center pane to see the available templates. In the category list, click **We've Moved**, and then click the **Compass Point** thumbnail.

2. Under **Customize** in the right pane, change the **Color scheme** to **Sapphire**, and under **Options**, change the **Side 2 information** to **Promotional text**. Then click **Create**.

   Publisher creates the postcard. If you have already saved text in an information set as we did in Chapter 1, your organization information appears on both sides of the postcard. You can customize the postcard using the techniques you learned in "Creating Folded Cards," earlier in this chapter.

3. Display page 2. Then on the **Tools** menu, point to **Mailings and Catalogs**, and click **Mail Merge**.

   Step 1 of the Mail Merge Wizard appears in the Mail Merge task pane.

4. With the **Use an existing list** option selected under **Create recipient list**, click **Next: Create or connect to a recipient list** at the bottom of the task pane.

5. In the **Select Data Source** dialog box, navigate to the *Documents\Microsoft Press\ SBS_Publisher2007\CardsCalendars* folder, and double-click the *DataSource* workbook.

   The Select Table dialog box opens.

6.  With the **Clients$** sheet and the **First row of data contains column headers** check box selected, click **OK**.

    The Mail Merge Recipients dialog box opens.

    If you use mail merge often, you will want to explore this dialog box to see how you can refine the mail merge process. For the purposes of this exercise, we will use the default settings.

7.  In the **Mail Merge Recipients** dialog box, click **OK**.

    Step 2 of the Mail Merge Wizard appears in the Mail Merge task pane, so that you can add data fields to your publication.

8.  In the postcard, click **Type address here** to select all the text in the address text box, and press the ⌨Del key. Then under **More items** in the task pane, click **Address block**.

    The Insert Address Block dialog box opens. From this dialog box, you can refine the format of the fields that constitute the name and address.

**Insert Address Block**

Specify address elements

☑ Insert recipient's name in this format:

Josh
Josh Randall Jr.
Josh Q. Randall Jr.
Joshua
Joshua Randall Jr.
Joshua Q. Randall Jr.

☑ Insert company name

☑ Insert postal address:

○ Never include the country/region in the address
○ Always include the country/region in the address
● Only include the country/region if different than:

United States

☑ Format address according to the destination country/region

Preview

Here is a preview from your recipient list:

1

Linda Martin
7899 38th St.
Tucker, NJ 90025

Correct Problems

If items in your address block are missing or out of order, use Match Fields to identify the correct address elements from your mailing list.

Match Fields...

OK    Cancel

9. Click **OK** to accept the default settings.

Publisher inserts the name and address of the first client in the data source into the text box.

10. To see the underlying data field, click the client's name.

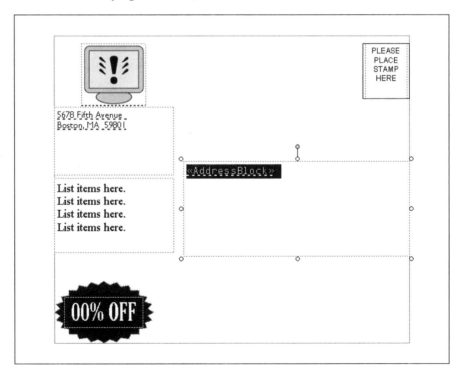

**11.** Display page 1, and insert a new text box below the **We've Moved** box.

**12.** Under **More items** in the task pane, click **Greeting line**.

The Insert Greeting Line dialog box opens so that you can specify how the greeting line should appear in the merged postcards.

**13.** Under **Greeting line format**, click the arrow to the right of the first box, and click **(none)**. Then click the arrow to the right of the second box, and toward the bottom of the list, click **Joshua**.

**14.** Under **Greeting line for invalid recipient names**, click **(none)**. Then click **OK**.

Publisher inserts the greeting line as it will appear for the first record in the data source file.

**15.** Click after the inserted comma (the name changes to display the data field), press [Space], and type don't miss our Open House on July 1. Then click away from the text box.

> **Troubleshooting** If <<GreetingLine>> is selected when you start to type, it will be overwritten by the first new character. If this happens, undo the change or delete the contents of the text box, and repeat Steps 13 through 15, this time ensuring that the insertion point is after <<GreetingLine>>.

The postcard is now ready for merging.

16. At the bottom of the **Mail Merge** task pane, click **Next: Create merged publication**.

    Step 3 of the Mail Merge Wizard appears in the Mail Merge task pane.

17. In the task pane, click **Merge to a new publication**. Then on the page sorter, click each page in turn to see the results.

    Publisher creates a publication that contains a personalized copy of the postcard for each of the five records in the data source. You can edit each copy as necessary in this publication before printing it. You can also save the publication for future use.

**CLOSE** the publication without saving your changes.

## Bulk Mail

If you do frequent large mailings of promotional materials or newsletters, you might want to look into *bulk mail*. The post office discounts the regular cost of postage to a bulk rate if your mailings are large enough (at least 500 pieces) and if you do some of the work necessary to sort and transport them.

To use bulk mail, you need to buy a permit ($175 a year as of this writing) from the bulk mailing center where you will deliver your mailings. You need to set up your publications within certain size and shape guidelines and either print postage permit information on the publications or use a postage meter. In addition, you need to maintain an accurate address list and sort and bundle your mailings by ZIP Code. In return for all that work, you can realize savings of at least $0.05 per piece, depending on the degree to which your mailings can be automated.

You can find out more about bulk mail and how to evaluate whether your mailings are worth the setup work by visiting

*www.usps.com/businessmail101/*

> **Tip**  Some copy and print shops provide *direct mail* services, meaning that they will merge your publication and data source while printing, sort the printed pieces, and then deliver them to the post office, ready for bulk mailing.

# Creating Calendars

Although various technologies are now available to track appointments and schedules electronically, many people still prefer to use printed calendars to keep them organized and on time. Calendars can be an excellent promotional item because they keep your information in front of the recipient for the entire calendar period. You can include information about promotions and events, or if you create a calendar for friends and family members, you can include information about personal events such as birthdays. You can use Publisher to create a calendar for a single month, for a range of months, or for an entire year. Various designs are available in full-page or wallet sizes, or you can build a custom-sized calendar from a blank publication.

After you choose a calendar template in the Getting Started window, you can specify whether each calendar page displays a month or a year, and which months or years the calendar includes. (If you don't select a year, Publisher creates a calendar for the current year.) Publisher creates a calendar consisting of one page specific to each month or year in the selected range. For example, setting a starting month of January and an ending month of June of the same year produces a six-page publication. You can also add a Schedule Of Events section, which is a text box next to the calendar grid on each page in which you can insert information. You can change the text box header to represent information other than events.

**See Also** You can insert a one-month calendar object from the Design Gallery into any type of publication. For information, see "Working with Pre-Designed Visual Elements" in Chapter 2, "Creating Visual Interest."

## Adding Captions, Credits, and Copyrights

Some calendar templates include placeholders for photographs or other artwork. If you are creating a calendar for distribution to other people and you select one of these templates, think carefully about the ownership of the artwork you plan on using. If you insert your own photographs, do you want to indicate ownership in some way? If you plan to use artwork created by other people, do you have the right to distribute those materials without infringing on the owner's rights?

Many people assume that if a graphic is available on the Web, it is part of the *public domain*. However, it is wise to err on the side of caution whenever you use artwork in your publications, unless you know it is not protected by a *copyright*. For example, the clip art that comes with Publisher and that is available from Microsoft Office Online is not copyrighted and can be used by anyone for any purpose. Materials that are copyrighted are usually accompanied by a variation of the following statement:

*Copyright © 2007 by Online Training Solutions, Inc. All rights reserved.*

If you want to use artwork that you have been given by someone else, it is wise to acknowledge the source. Otherwise, hard feelings can result if it appears to the owner that you are trying to claim credit for his or her work. You can add captions, credits, and copyrights to your publications in unobtrusive text boxes, so don't be tempted to omit them only because you think they might detract from your design.

## Changing the Background

In Publisher, you can customize the *background* of any page by adding a solid color, a color gradient, a texture, or even a picture. This type of formatting is particularly effective in full-page publications such as calendars, because the background holds the objects on the page together with a cohesive design element.

A *color gradient* is a visual effect in which a solid color gradually changes from light to dark or dark to light. Publisher offers several gradient patterns, each with several variations. You can also choose a preset arrangement of colors from professionally designed backgrounds in which different colors gradually merge.

> **Tip** Be cautious when using preset color arrangements with calendars. It is important that the background be subtle and that it not compete with the other objects for attention or make them unreadable.

If you want something fancier than a gradient, you can give the background a *texture*, or you can even use a picture. Publisher comes with several textures that you can easily apply to the background of your pages.

## Working with the Master Page

When you create a publication, the pages take on the characteristics of the template on which it is based. You can then make changes to individual pages. In a multi-page publication, making the same change to the design of every page can be tedious. For efficiency and precision, you can make the change to the publication's *master page* instead.

The design of the master page controls the look of all the pages in the publication. Anything that appears on the master page appears on every page. Most master page elements can be changed only on the master page. (An exception is the background; you can override a master page background on an individual publication page.) For this reason, most publications created with Publisher templates have a blank master page—the design elements are individually inserted on each page so that you can easily change them.

To make changes to a publication's master page, you click Master Page on the View menu to display the page, the Edit Master Pages task pane, and the Edit Master Pages toolbar.

By clicking buttons on the toolbar, you can do the following:

- Add a new master page.
- Duplicate or rename the active master page, or delete it if there is more than one.
- Add layout guides to the active master page.

    **See Also**  For information about layout guides, see "Using Guides" in Chapter 4, "Marketing Your Product, Service, or Organization."

- Display spreads or single pages.

Clicking the Close Master View button on the toolbar returns you to the publication. You can temporarily display the publication's pages to check the effects of a change by clicking View Publication Pages at the bottom of the Edit Master Pages task pane.

While the master page is displayed, you can choose commands from menus and click buttons on toolbars to insert and format the elements you want to appear on every page of the publication. For example, you might want to add your company logo or a watermark to every page.

In this exercise, you will first create a full-page calendar for the entire year, with a custom photograph and copyright statement. You will then create a 12-page calendar with a schedule of events for the current month, change the background of an individual page, and then change the background on the master page.

**USE** the *Arizona10* picture. This practice file is located in the *Documents\Microsoft Press\ SBS_Publisher2007\CardsCalendars* folder.

**BE SURE TO** display the Getting Started window before beginning this exercise.

1. In the **Publication Types** list, click **Calendars**, and then scroll the center pane to see the broad range of available design templates.

2. In the **Full Page** category, click **Photo Album**.

3. Under **Customize** in the right pane, set the **Color scheme** to **Aqua**. Under **Options**, change the **Page size** to **Portrait** and the **Timeframe** to **One year per page**. Then click **Create**.

   Publisher creates a full-page, vertical, 12-month calendar based on the selected design template.

4. Zoom to **100%**, and scroll to the top of the page.

5. Right-click the existing picture, point to **Change Picture**, and then click **From File**. In the **Insert Picture** dialog box, navigate to the *Documents\Microsoft Press\ SBS_Publisher2007\CardsCalendars* folder, and double-click the *Arizona10* picture.

   **See Also** For information about inserting and manipulating pictures, see "Working with Graphics" in Chapter 2, "Creating Visual Interest."

Text Box

6. On the **Objects** toolbar, click the **Text Box** button, and then draw a text box below the photograph. Make it the width of the photograph and about a quarter inch high.

7. In the text box, type Copyright (c) 2006 by Barry Preppernau. All rights reserved.

   > **Tip** When you press the Spacebar after typing *(c)*, Publisher substitutes the copyright symbol, because the Replace Text As You Type check box is selected in the AutoCorrect dialog box. For information about AutoCorrect, see "Correcting Spelling Errors" in Chapter 5, "Creating Text-Based Publications."

   Because some text will not fit in the text box, Publisher displays the Text In Overflow button.

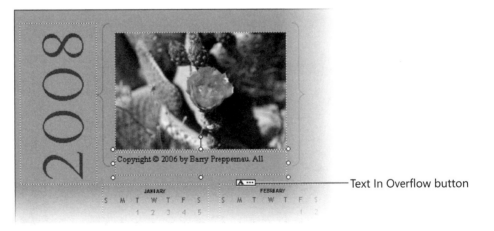

Text In Overflow button

   **See Also** For information about ways to work with overflow text, see "Continuing Stories from One Text Box to Another" in Chapter 4, "Marketing Your Product, Service, or Organization."

Decrease
Font Size

8. Press Ctrl + A to select all the text in the text box, and then on the **Formatting** toolbar, click the **Decrease Font Size** button until all the text you typed fits on one line. Then click an empty area of the page to see the results.

Copyright © 2006 by Barry Preppernau. All rights reserved

**9.** Repeat steps 1 through 3 to create a calendar with the Axis design and the Waterfall color scheme. Under Options in the right pane, click **Set Calendar Dates**, set the **Start date** to **January** and the **End date** to **December**, and click **OK**. Select the **Include schedule of events** check box, and then click **Create**.

Publisher creates a 12-page, horizontal calendar.

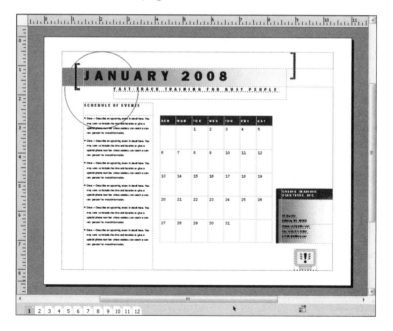

Other
Task Panes

**10.** On the title bar of the **Format Publication** task pane, click the **Other Task Panes** button, and then click **Background** to display the Background task pane.

**11.** Click several options to see their effects on the calendar.

Clicking one of the color boxes at the top of the task pane changes the gradients at the top of the More Colors list to reflect that color. You can also apply any of the available textures, patterns, or pictures to the calendar's background.

**12.** In the **Background** task pane, directly under **Apply a background**, click the **30% tint of Accent 1** (violet) square. Then click any gradient fill box in the list.

**13.** On the page sorter, click several pages to verify that the background was applied to only the first calendar page. Then redisplay page 1.

**14.** On the **View** menu, click **Master Page** to display the publication's underlying master page.

**15.** Display the **Background** task pane, and at the bottom, click **More backgrounds**. Then under **Colors** on the **Gradient** tab of the **Fill Effects** dialog box, click **Two colors**.

The Fill Effects dialog box changes to display the options for two-color gradients.

> **Tip** You can also use the Fill Effects dialog box to apply a gradient fill to objects such as text boxes. Simply click the Fill Color arrow on the Formatting toolbar, and then click Fill Effects.

**16.** Click the **Color 2** arrow, and click the **Accent 2** (aqua) square. Then under **Shading styles**, click **From corner**, and under **Variants**, click the lower-left box. Click **OK**.

**17.** At the top of the **Background** task pane, click the **Other Task Panes** button, and click **Edit Master Pages** to display that task pane. Then at the bottom of the pane, click **View publication pages**. Then click various pages on the page sorter.

The master page background has been applied to all the pages, but the background you applied directly to page 1 in step 12 is still visible in parts of that page.

**18.** Display page 1, display the **Background** task pane, and click the **No Fill** box at the top of the first column in the list.

The additional background is removed from page 1 so that it displays the entire master page background.

**CLOSE** the open publications without saving your changes.

# Packaging Publications for Printing

The simplest way to submit your publication to a copy shop, print shop, or online print service is as a *Portable Document Format (PDF) file*. You can create a PDF file from Publisher without purchasing special software by installing the Microsoft Save As PDF Or XPS add-in from the Microsoft Office Online Downloads site. You can then use the Pack And Go command to create a PDF file that includes all the information a professional printer needs when printing your publication.

In this exercise, you will install the Microsoft Save As PDF Or XPS add-in, and then use the Pack And Go command to create a PDF file that you can submit to a printer.

> **USE** the *Postcard* publication. This practice file is located in the *Documents\Microsoft Press\SBS_Publisher2007\CardsCalendars* folder.
>
> **BE SURE TO** have an active Internet connection before beginning this exercise.

1. Start your default Internet browser, and go to *office.microsoft.com/en-us/downloads/*.

2. In the left pane, under **By Version**, click **2007 Office System**, click **2007 Microsoft Office System**, and then click **Add-ins**.

3. In the list of add-ins, click **2007 Microsoft Office Add-in: Microsoft Save As PDF or XPS**.

4. On the installation page, click **Continue**. After the Genuine Advantage Tool confirms that you are running genuine, licensed software, click **Install** and follow the installation instructions given.

   > **Troubleshooting** You might need to install the Genuine Advantage Tool before you can proceed.

5. After the installation completes, navigate to the *Documents\Microsoft Press\SBS_Publisher2007\CardsCalendars* folder, and then double-click the *Postcard* publication.

   Notice that the graphic in the lower-left corner of this postcard extends beyond the active area of the publication; we'll explain why in a minute.

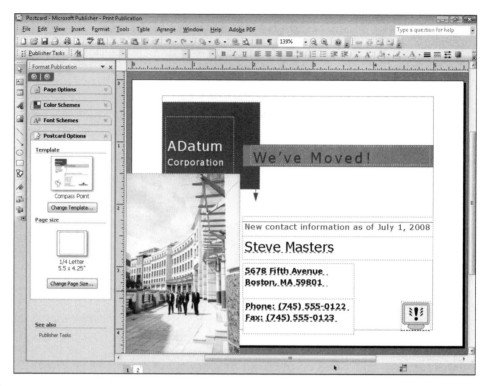

6. On the **File** menu, point to **Pack and Go**, and then click **Take to a Commercial Printing Service**.

The Take To A Commercial Printing Service task pane opens. At the bottom of the pane, Publisher indicates that it will create both a PDF file and a .pub file when you click Save to complete the process.

If you are going to print thousands of postcards by the four-color printing method, you need to change the publication from RGB color mode to CMYK color mode. But provided your local copy or print shop offers digital printing, you can ignore the issue flagged in the Select An Item To Fix box.

**See Also** For information about CMYK colors, see the sidebar titled "Color Models," earlier in this chapter.

**7.** In the task pane, click **Printing Options**.

The Print Options dialog box opens.

A copy or print shop might tell you to include crop marks or bleed marks in the PDF file. *Crop marks* are used when a publication is printed on a sheet of paper that is larger than the desired output. They appear in the four corners of a publication to indicate where the printer should trim the pages. A *bleed* is an element that appears to extend partially beyond the edge of the page, like the photograph in the lower-left corner of the postcard. The extent of the bleed is indicated by the *bleed marks*.

**8.** With **One page per sheet** selected in the **Printing options** box, click **OK**.

The copy or print shop usually requires this setting for compatibility with its own printing software.

**9.** At the bottom of the task pane, click **Save**.

> **Troubleshooting**  If you have not yet saved a publication, a message appears prompting you to do so. Click OK in the message box. Then in the Save As dialog box, assign a name to the publication, and save it in the *Documents\Microsoft Press\ SBS_Publisher2007\CardsCalendars* folder.

The Pack And Go Wizard starts, and asks where you want to save the publication package.

> **Pack and Go Wizard**
>
> **Select the location for saving your files**
>
> Where would you like to pack your publication to?
>
> ◉ Burn to disc on D:\
> ○ Copy to removable storage on F:\
> ○ Copy to floppy disk on A:\
> ○ Other location:   [                    ]   [ Browse... ]
>
> [ < Back ]   [ Next > ]   [ Cancel ]   [ Finish ]

**10.** Insert a blank CD in your CD burner, and with **Burn to disc on D:\** (or the equivalent drive on your computer) selected, click **Next**.

If your computer does not have a CD burner, click the Other Location option instead, and then browse to the folder in which you want to store the package.

> **Tip**  Publisher 2007 does not support the direct burning of content to a DVD. If you prefer to burn to a DVD rather than a CD, package your publication to a folder on your computer, and then use DVD-burning software to create the DVD.

**11.** When the wizard announces that your publication is successfully packed, clear the **Print a composite proof** check box, and then click **OK**.

Publisher creates a compressed file on the CD (or in the designated folder) containing a PDF file and a .pub file. You can take the compressed file to the copy or print shop for printing.

**CLOSE** the open publications without saving your changes, and if you are not continuing on to the next chapter, quit Publisher.

> ### Binding
>
> If you want to produce a calendar as a give-away promotion for clients or as a gift for family and friends, you will probably want to print multiple copies of the calendar pages in color on stiff paper or card stock. As you prepare the calendar, bear in mind the issues discussed in "Printing Both Sides of Thick Paper," earlier in this chapter. With annual calendars, an additional consideration is the method you will use for binding the 12 calendar pages to create an attractive package.
>
> If you print your calendar at a copy or print shop, you usually have several binding options, including comb, wire, and coil. All of these options create a professional look and allow the pages to lie flat; however, they come at a price. Depending on the quantity you purchase, comb binding can be $3 or more per calendar, and coil binding can be $4 or more.
>
> You might also talk to a customer service representative about *stapling*, also called *saddle-stitching*, which is a good option for wallet-size calendars. Stapling involves printing the calendar on three sheets of sturdy paper with two pages on each side. The sheets are then collated, stapled in the middle, and folded to create a booklet. This is considerably cheaper than other binding methods.

# Key Points

- With so many templates to choose from, you can save time by selecting the one that is closest in size and layout to the publication you want.

- Although all the templates come with a default color scheme, you can switch to a different scheme at any time. And you can expand the scheme by adding custom colors.

- Printing is a big consideration whenever you need more than just a few copies of a publication. Design with the printing method—and your budget—in mind.

- If you need to send a publication to a large group of people, save time by merging their contact information directly into the publication.

- Subtle backgrounds can unify a publication. In a multi-page publication, the background belongs on the master page.

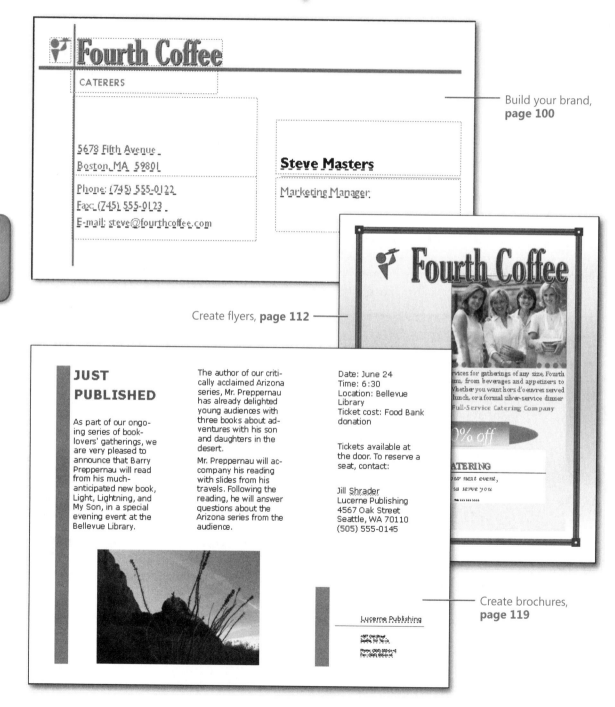

Build your brand, **page 100**

Create flyers, **page 112**

Create brochures, **page 119**

# 4 Marketing Your Product, Service, or Organization

**In this chapter, you will learn to:**

✔ Build your brand.

✔ Create flyers.

✔ Create brochures.

To market your product, service, or organization to customers, clients, and members, you will often need to produce eye-catching printed materials. In fact, every written communication should build confidence in your company or organization by representing you in a professional, stylish way.

Even if you want to create materials such as flyers and brochures for personal reasons, you can still benefit from the ideas and techniques discussed in this chapter. Whether you are creating a flyer to appeal for information about a lost pet or a brochure to announce a sports team's practice times and game schedules, we will give you the skills you need to produce a well-designed, carefully laid out publication.

In this chapter, we start with a discussion of ways to build a brand through the consistent presentation of printed materials such as business cards, letterhead, envelopes, and business forms. Then we demonstrate how to use Microsoft Office Publisher 2007 to create flyers and brochures, both by using the many templates provided by Publisher for this purpose and from your own creativity. In the process, you learn more about formatting, design, and layout.

**See Also** Do you need only a quick refresher on the topics in this chapter? See the Quick Reference entries on pages xxvii–xli.

**Important** Before you can use the practice files in this chapter, you need to install them from the book's companion CD to their default location. See "Using the Book's CD" on page xvii for more information.

**Troubleshooting** Graphics and operating system–related instructions in this book reflect the Windows Vista user interface. If your computer is running Windows XP and you experience trouble following the instructions as written, please refer to the "Information for Readers Running Windows XP" section at the beginning of this book.

# Building Your Brand

The *brand* of a company or organization is its identity. It includes the name and logo, the fonts and colors used in materials sent to customers or members, and the design of those materials. It even encompasses the feeling you want the people you deal with to have about the product or service you provide. For maximum effect, your brand should be evident on all the materials you use to communicate with your customers or members, such as your business card, printed and electronic letterhead, envelopes, Web site, and product packaging, and on business forms such as applications, estimates, invoices, purchase orders, and statements of account. This helps to build and maintain brand awareness.

Large companies spend hundreds of thousands of dollars annually establishing their brand by means of advertising and media campaigns. The desired result is a brand that is recognized by potential customers and elicits certain assumptions and expectations about the company or product. Some brands, such as Microsoft and Disney, use the company name to evoke a response, whereas others, such as McDonalds (the golden arches) and Nike (the swoosh), use a trademarked icon to connect with their customers.

**See Also** For information about trademarks, see the sidebar titled "Trademarks and Service Marks," later in this chapter.

You might never engage in an advertising campaign with the sole purpose of building brand recognition. But that doesn't mean you shouldn't pay close attention to the identity you create and what it says about you. Your brand can be a valuable marketing tool, and to the extent that you succeed in identifying your brand with products or services that people want, it can be a valuable asset. Even a local organization such as a homeowners' association or children's playgroup can benefit from a brand that instantly identifies the source of materials and their importance to their recipients.

## Company or Organization Names

If you are just forming your company or organization, you will need to assign it a unique name, both to register the entity with the state and to distinguish it from other companies providing a similar product or service. If possible, the name should convey instantly what the company or organization does in all the environments where it is likely to appear. Here are some do's and don'ts:

- Ensure that you can register your company or organization name as a domain name. Even if you don't intend to set up a Web site or a dedicated e-mail address right now, you might want to do so in the future, so it is wise to register a domain name that corresponds to your company or organization name from the very beginning.

- Browse through printed and online phone books to determine how you would search for a particular product or service. You might decide to make your product or service the first word of the name. For example, if your organization supplies public-service information about solar energy, you might want to begin its name with the word *Solar.*

- If no particular word defines your company, you might want to begin the first word of its name with a letter from the beginning of the alphabet so that it appears early in lists of similar companies or organizations. However, avoid clichés such as *AAA* or *Acme.*

- Avoid starting the name with the article *A*, *An*, or *The*; it might result in your company or organization being listed in places where people might not think to look for it. Similarly, avoid using digits at the beginning of the name.

- Avoid words that are difficult to spell or to pronounce.

- Choose a name that includes at least one unusual or out-of-context word, to make it more memorable.

- If you will be operating in an international setting, or in a culturally diverse environment, ask a native speaker of the prevailing language(s) to give you feedback on your choice of name and logo. Some words or symbols in English can be derogatory or unintentionally funny to a person from a different background or have an unintended meaning in another language.

## Trademarks and Service Marks

If your name or logo uniquely identifies your company or its products or services, you might want to register it as a *trademark* or *service mark* to establish your exclusive right to use it. A trademark is intended to identify the source of a product, and a service mark the source of a service; however, the terms "trademark" and "mark" are commonly used to refer to both trademarks and service marks. You can trademark not only names and logos, but also words, sounds, and colors. In general, you cannot trademark a common word or phrase, and a trademark is usually enforceable only for a specific type of products or services in a particular industry.

> **Tip**  Trademarks are not the same as *copyrights* and *patents*, which protect the ownership of artistic or literary works and inventions, respectively. For information about copyrights, visit *lcweb.loc.gov/copyright/*. For information about patents, visit *www.uspto.gov/main/patents.htm*.

You apply for trademark registration through the United States Patent and Trademark Office at *www.uspto.gov/main/trademarks.htm*. (Conversely, before you start using a logo, you can use the same site to check whether it is already registered to another company.)

The process of registering a trademark, which involves legal review and publication for opposition in the Official Gazette, takes at least six months to complete and costs $275 or more. Until the process is complete, you can designate your logo with a trademark ™ or service mark SM symbol to indicate that you claim ownership. After the trademark is registered, you can designate the logo with the registered trademark symbol ®. Then if anyone uses your trademark without your permission in connection with a similar type of product or service, you can enforce your ownership in a court of law.

Many trademark applications are filed each year by people who think they might eventually want to use the trademarked item. If you do not actively use the logo for an extended period of time or if you do not actively enforce the trademark by responding to violations, your ownership of the trademark can be terminated. To guard against this, you should include the registered trademark symbol with all uses of the logo, and your publications should include notices asserting your ownership of the trademark.

## Creating a Logo

A *logo* is a graphic or text or a combination of the two that identifies a company or organization—or its products or services—in a unique way. It is used in addition to or instead of the name in printed and online materials and is part of the effort to present those materials in a consistent way that promotes brand recognition.

Because your logo represents your company or organization and will probably be used in different ways, bear in mind the following when designing your logo:

- You want to distinguish yourself from your competitors with a tasteful, memorable design.
- The logo should be recognizable at a glance, which rules out most photographs or complex graphics.
- The logo should be flexible enough to work in several sizes (such as tiny on a business card and large on the side of a delivery van).
- It should work in black and white or in color. Limit the number of colors, and avoid gradients that might be hard to render in processes such as *silk-screening*.
- It should work on hard surfaces (such as building signs) or soft surfaces (such as T-shirts).
- Unless your company or organization is associated with a specific culture or religion, your logo should avoid images or fonts that imply such connections.

If you don't have graphic skills or access to a graphics program in which to create a logo, you can design one by using a base layout from the Design Gallery and then adding elements such as shapes, WordArt, and regular text. You can also find logo-design services and do-it-yourself logo design programs online.

**See Also** For information about inserting elements from the Design Gallery into a publication, see "Working with Pre-Designed Visual Elements" in Chapter 2, "Creating Visual Interest."

## Choosing a Font Scheme

In Chapter 3, "Creating Colorful Cards and Calendars," you learned how to vary the look of a publication by changing the color scheme. Color can be an important component of your brand. Equally important is the combination of fonts you use. Publisher makes it easy to experiment with font combinations by providing an extensive library of font schemes. These schemes consist of a compatible heading font and body-text font that, in conjunction with the color schemes, provide you with many ready-made ways to change the look and mood of a publication.

As with color schemes, you can assign a font scheme to a publication as you create it in the Getting Started window. In an existing publication, you can switch to a different font scheme in the Font Scheme area of the Format Publication task pane. You can also apply fonts from outside of the current font scheme to selected text by clicking the font you want in the Font list on the Formatting toolbar.

**See Also**  For more information about font schemes, see "Solving Organization Problems" in Chapter 5, "Creating Text-Based Publications."

Of course, you are not limited to the font combinations provided by Publisher. You can format selected text or styles with a non-scheme font at any time.

**See Also**  For information about varying the look of a font by changing character attributes, see "Formatting Text for Visual Impact" in Chapter 2, "Creating Visual Interest."

## Adding Items to the Content Library

You can store text or graphics that you might want to use in more than one publication in the Content Library. You can use an item from the library as-is or insert it from the library and then modify it, instead of having to create it manually. For example, suppose you combine a graphic and text to create an attractive element that advertises your Web site. You can store the element in the Content Library so that you can use it in other publications.

In this exercise, you will first create an envelope and a custom logo, and then select colors and a font scheme to establish consistent branding. You store the logo in the Content Library, and then create a coordinating business card by adapting the logo and applying the chosen design, color, and font for a consistent look.

> **USE** the *Icon* and *Name* graphics and the *BusinessCard, Envelope,* and *Invoice*
> publications. These practice files are located in the *Documents\Microsoft Press\*
> *SBS_Publisher2007\MarketingMaterials* folder.
>
> **BE SURE TO** start Publisher and display the Getting Started window before beginning
> this exercise.

1. In the **Publication Types** list, click **Envelopes**, and scroll the center pane to get an idea of the range of available designs.

2. In the **Classic Designs** category, click **Crossed Lines**. Under **Options** in the right pane, set the **Color scheme** to **Waterfall** and clear the **Include logo** check box. Then click **Create**.

   Publisher creates an envelope with the selected design, and inserts the company name and return address from the active information set.

3. Click the border of the blue text box, and press the ⌈Del⌋ key. Then click either of the blue lines, and press ⌈Del⌋.

   Because the two line objects were grouped, selecting and deleting one of the lines deletes both of them. The envelope design now includes only the return address and the address area.

Design Gallery
Object

4. On the **Objects** toolbar, click the **Design Gallery Object** button, and in the left pane of the **Design Gallery**, click **Logos**. If necessary, enlarge the gallery window by dragging its border so you can see the logos in the center pane.

5. In the center pane, under **Additional designs**, click **Crossed Corner**. In the **Options** pane, experiment with the **Graphic** and **Lines of text** options, observing the changes to the design thumbnails. Finish with **Graphic**, set to **Include**, and **Lines of text** set to 2. Then click **Insert Object**.

   Publisher inserts a logo containing a placeholder graphic (in the shape of a pyramid) and placeholder text (Organization Name) in the center of the envelope.

6. Drag the logo to the return address area in the upper-left corner of the envelope, and then change the **Zoom** level to 200%.

7. On the **Arrange** menu, click **Ungroup**, and then click a blank area of the publication to release the selection.

   You can now change the individual logo elements.

**See Also** For information about grouped objects, see "Connecting and Grouping Shapes" in Chapter 2, "Creating Visual Interest."

**8.** In the return address area, select and delete the pyramid, select and delete the **Organization** text box, and change the word **Name** to Caterers.

Notice that the font of the word *Name* is formatted as All Caps, and this formatting is automatically transferred to the word *Caterers*.

**9.** On the **Objects** bar, click **Picture Frame**, and then click **Picture from File**. Drag to draw a frame in the empty space to the right of the return address. In the **Insert Picture** dialog box, navigate to the *Documents\Microsoft Press\SBS_Publisher2007\ MarketingMaterials* folder, and double-click the *Name* graphic. Move the inserted company name graphic to the upper-right quadrant of the crossed lines. Then move and size the graphic to fill the width of the quadrant.

**10.** Repeat step 9 to insert the *Icon* graphic in the upper-left quadrant, sizing it to about the same height as the name.

**11.** Change the color of both lines to **Accent 2** and the color of the word *Caterers* to **Orange** (by selecting it from the More Colors palette). Then move the **Caterers** text box, to left-align the word *Caterers* with the word *Fourth*.

> **Troubleshooting** To select the text box rather than the text it contains, click its border.

**12.** Select the two graphics, one text box, and two lines that form the new envelope logo (hold down the ⎡Shift⎤ key as you click each one), and group them.

**13.** Right-click the group, and then click **Add to Content Library**.

The Add Item To Content Library dialog box opens.

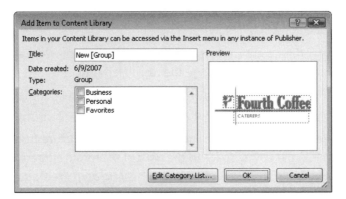

14. In the **Title** box, type Fourth Coffee Logo. In the **Categories** box, select the **Business** check box. Then click **OK** to store the item in the Content Library.

> **Tip** You can create, delete, rename, and reorder categories by clicking Edit Category List.

The Content Library task pane opens, displaying a thumbnail of the item.

15. On the envelope, click inside the text box containing the return address, press `Ctrl`+`A` to select all the text, and then change the font color to **Accent 2**.

Other Task Panes

16. In the **Content Library** task pane, click the **Other Task Panes** button, and then click **Format Publication**. In the **Format Publication** task pane, expand the **Font Schemes** area.

17. In the **Zoom** list, click **Whole Page**. Then click various font schemes to see the effect on the publication, noticing that all the text in the envelope publication changes to reflect your selection. Finish by selecting the **Facet** scheme.

    The envelope is complete. Now create a business card to match.

18. Display the **Getting Started** window, and create a business card with the **Crossed Lines** design, the **Waterfall** color scheme, the **Facet** font scheme, and no logo. Then delete the blue text box, and ungroup the blue lines.

Item from
Content Library

19. On the **Objects** toolbar, click the **Item from Content Library** button. In the **Content Library** task pane, point to the **Fourth Coffee Logo** item, click the arrow that appears, and then click **Insert**. Drag the inserted logo to the upper-left corner of the business card, and then ungroup the logo object.

> **Tip** If you have many items in your Content Library, you can search for a particular item based on various properties such as category, type, and date of creation.

20. Delete the green vertical and horizontal lines from the inserted logo. Move the vertical blue line to the right and the horizontal blue line down, to replace the green lines. Then change the color of the lines to **Accent 2**.

21. Select and group the two graphics, one text box, and two lines that form the business card logo, and then add the logo to the Content Library.

22. Move the two text boxes containing the contact information to the right, to align the left edge of each box with the vertical line, and up, to center-align with the name and title boxes to the right.

23. Decrease the font size of the address and contact details to **6 pt**, to bring the e-mail address into view. Change the font color of the address and contact details, and the line color of the line between the name and title to **Accent 2**, and change the font color of the title to **Orange**.

Reducing the font size brings additional content into view.

**24.** Use the techniques you have learned to create other items that coordinate with the business card and envelope you created in this exercise. For tips, refer to the *BusinessCard, Envelope,* and *Invoice* publications in the *Documents\Microsoft Press\ SBS_Publisher2007\MarketingMaterials* folder.

**CLOSE** the open publications without saving your changes.

### Résumés

At one time or another, most people find themselves in the position of having to market themselves. To convince other people that they need to "buy" what you have to offer, you might want to consider developing a personal brand that includes letterhead, envelopes, a business card, and—most important—a résumé, all with the same professional look.

Publisher offers three categories of résumé templates: Entry Level, Chronological, and Curriculum Vitae. Each category has three designs, with the full range of color schemes and font schemes available. After you create the résumé publication, you can customize it with graphic elements of your own choosing.

As you add information to your résumé, bear in mind that although an attractive design with matching cover letter and envelope might on the surface be an indication of a professional attitude, nothing will offset careless typing mistakes. So be sure to spell-check and then proofread your résumé and cover letter carefully before distributing them. To be on the safe side, ask someone else to proofread it also; a second set of eyes will often catch mistakes that you don't see because you are familiar with the content. If your assistant proofreader happens to work with the same type of organization you're marketing yourself to, he or she might be able to offer helpful insights into the content and impact of your résumé.

These documents represent examples of your desktop publishing skills. If you will be distributing them electronically, it is important that you demonstrate good techniques. For example, a common error we find in résumés submitted to us in Microsoft Office Word document format is the use of multiple tabs, spaces, or a combination of tabs and spaces to position an item on the page. This clearly demonstrates that the applicant does not have the basic Word skills that are vital within our organization.

**See Also** For information about checking spelling, see "Correcting Spelling Errors" in Chapter 5, "Creating Text-Based Publications."

# Creating Flyers

Flyers are one-page, one-sided publications that are designed to be read at a glance. Don't underestimate the task of designing a good flyer; you need to distill the information down to the minimum number of words that will convey your message and arrange the text along with graphics for maximum impact.

Publisher comes with many flyer templates. Some present different designs for marketing a product, service, or event; others are special-purpose layouts for sales, fundraisers, or announcements. Instead of using one of these templates, however, in this section we show you how to arrange elements created by using the techniques you learned in earlier chapters to create a flyer on a blank page. This process is called *page layout*.

---

### Event Programs

Although Publisher templates are organized into categories, you can and should consider many of them as starting points for a multitude of publication types. You can personalize any publication you create based on a template. Some Publisher templates are more specifically targeted. For example, if your organization presents information through public performances or gatherings, you might find it convenient to create programs to share information about each presentation by using Publisher.

Publisher 2007 includes three preformatted programs, ostensibly designed for musical performances, theater performances, and religious services, but certainly applicable to other types of gatherings. Each program begins as a four-page publication and provides structured areas for an overview and breakdown of the event, names and roles of participants, and other information you might want to share with attendees.

---

## Using Guides

After inserting graphics and text boxes or drawing shapes in approximate locations on a blank page, you can precisely position, align, and stack the objects by using the commands on the Arrange menu. In addition to the blue margin guides, three other types of non-printing guides help you precisely position and align objects:

- *Grid guides*. You display these fixed lines to create a grid on the page for use when laying out a publication. You can specify how many column guides and row guides you want, as well as the spacing between them.

**See Also** For information about layout grids, see the sidebar titled "Page Layout and the Grid," later in this chapter.

● *Baseline guides*. You display these fixed horizontal lines to show baselines to align text you have in your publication. This is useful if you want to align the text in multiple text boxes.

● *Ruler guides*. You display these movable horizontal and vertical lines when you want to precisely position or align objects without using a grid.

## Aligning and Stacking Objects

Clicking Align Or Distribute on the Arrange menu gives you access to commands for aligning individual or multiple objects in several ways. For example, you can:

● Align objects vertically so that their left or right edge or centerline aligns with that of the first object selected. Or align them horizontally so that their top or bottom edge or centerline aligns with that of the first object selected.

● Distribute multiple objects evenly within the space they currently occupy, either horizontally or vertically.

● Align objects with the page margins, or distribute them evenly between the page margins.

You can also have objects that you move automatically *snap* (attach themselves) to the nearest ruler mark, guide, or other object.

When objects overlap each other, they are *stacked*. The stacking order is determined by the order in which you inserted the object, with the first object at the bottom of the stack and the last object at the top. You can change the stacking order by bringing an object to the top (the front) of the stack, sending it to the bottom (the back), or moving it forward or backward one position at a time.

If you can't locate or select an object because it is covered by others in the stack, you can run the Design Checker to identify hidden objects. You can then click Go To This Item or Bring Object To Front to make the object accessible.

**Tip** The Design Checker detects design problems in your publications, such as objects that are not within the print area or are off the page, text boxes containing more text than can be displayed, and pictures that are disproportionately scaled.

When you have many objects to organize on a page, it is often helpful to remove some of them temporarily so that you have room to work. Publisher provides a gray *scratch area* around the page in which you can place an object until you decide where it fits. When you want to move an object to a different page of a multi-page publication, it is often more convenient to move an object to the scratch area, display the page where it belongs, and then move the object onto that page than it is to cut and paste the object.

## Page Layout and the Grid

Professionally designed brochures, newsletters, newspapers, and books are built on an invisible skeleton called a *grid*. The grid is a system of columns and rows, sometimes with spaces called *alleys* between them, that imposes a logical layout on the content of the publication and provides visual continuity from one page to the next. Using a grid speeds up the layout process by making it easier to decide where to place various objects.

After you set the margins of a publication, defining a grid divides the space within the margins into *grid units*. The optimum number of units is determined by the purpose of the publication and the number and type of elements to be included in your layout. The more different types and different sizes of elements, the more grid units you might need to accommodate them. The grid units help you place the objects and ensure that you size objects proportionally.

There are no hard and fast rules about which grid you should use for which type of publication, but many designers find that it is best to create a grid with an odd number of units both horizontally and vertically. This type of grid provides a structure that is flexible enough to accommodate most types of text and graphics. For example, a three by three grid (nine grid units arranged in three columns and three rows) can accommodate three columns of text or one column that spans one grid unit and another column that spans two. Similarly, a heading can span one, two, or three columns. You can size a graphic to occupy any number of grid units, and it will remain proportional to the other elements on the page.

For small publications such as postcards, you might not need a grid, but for longer publications, using a grid will help you produce a more sophisticated look. And if visual continuity between a set of different types of publications is important, using the same grid for them all is a must.

In this exercise, you will align objects in various ways, change their stacking order, and position them with the help of a grid.

> **USE** the *Flyer* publication. This practice file is located in the *Documents\Microsoft Press\ SBS_Publisher2007\MarketingMaterials* folder.
>
> **OPEN** the *Flyer* publication.

1. Set the **Zoom** level to **Whole Page**.

2. On the **Tools** menu, click **Design Checker**.

   The Design Checker notifies you of a hidden object.

> **Tip** Depending on the default printer installed on your computer, Design Checker might also notify you that an object is in the nonprintable region of the page. We're not going to be printing this flyer, so you can ignore this flag if it appears in the Design Checker task pane.

3. In the **Design Checker** task pane, point to the **Object is not visible** warning, click the arrow that appears, and then click **Fix: Bring Object to Front**.

   The logo graphic is now visible at the top of the stack of objects.

4. Drag the logo into the gray scratch area to the left of the page.

5. Close the **Design Checker** task pane. Then drag the photograph into the scratch area to the right of the page.

6. On the **Arrange** menu, click **Layout Guides**, and then in the **Layout Guides** dialog box, click the **Grid Guides** tab.

   You can set column guides and row guides, as well as the space between them.

7. Under **Column Guides**, change the **Columns** setting to 5, and under **Row Guides**, change the **Rows** setting to 7. Then click **OK**.

A grid of squares with a 0.2 inch space between each column and each row now occupies the entire space between the blue margin guides.

8. Right-click the visible part of the **Fourth Coffee** heading, point to **Order**, and then click **Bring to Front**.

   You might need to move the WordArt toolbar to see the object.

9. With **Fourth Coffee** still selected, on the **Arrange** menu, point to **Align or Distribute**, and then click **Relative to Margin Guides** to turn on that option.

10. On the **Arrange** menu, point to **Align or Distribute**, and click **Align Top**. Then point to **Align or Distribute**, and click **Align Right**.

11. Now drag the lower-left corner handle down and to the left to stretch the object until it fills four of the five grid units at the top of the page.

12. Click the coupon object, and drag it toward the lower-right corner of the page. Stop dragging when the object snaps to align with the bottom and right margin guides.

    The object snaps to the guides because To Guides is turned on under Snap on the Arrange menu.

    > **Tip** If you want the freedom to position an object without snapping, hold down the Alt key as you drag the object.

13. Drag the row of orange dots out of the way, and then enlarge the coupon until it fills the bottom three grid rows across the five grid columns.

**14.** Drag the text box down until it slightly overlaps the coupon, and then drag the row of dots until it sits immediately above the text box.

Now you can arrange the objects currently stored in the scratch area.

**15.** Drag the photograph onto the page, aligning the right edge with the right margin and aligning the top edge so that *Fourth Coffee* does not obscure the women's faces. Then hold down the shift key and drag the lower-left corner handle to enlarge the photo until it spans the right three grid units.

**16.** With the photo still selected, on the **Arrange** menu, point to **Order**, and then click **Send to Back**.

The photo moves behind the other objects on the page.

**17.** Drag the logo onto the page, and then align it with the left and top margin guides.

**18.** Click a blank area of the page, and then on the **View** menu, click **Boundaries and Guides** to turn off that option.

Publisher hides the margin and grid guides so that you can see the results of your work.

**CLOSE** the *Flyer* publication without saving your changes.

# Creating Brochures

Brochures are one-page, two-sided publications that are designed to be folded to create four or six panels. The outside page of the brochure is the "wrapper." The front panel usually displays the brochure's title, and the back panel often has contact details and a place for a mailing address. The other panels might contain information about the company or organization. The real message of the brochure is carried on the three or four panels on the inside page. When the brochure is opened, all the panels on this page can be viewed at once, so they are generally designed to create a harmonious balance and a smooth flow of information.

Publisher comes with many brochure templates. Some present information in various formats that you customize to meet your needs. Some include space for general information but also include a structured price list in a tabular format. Eight special-purpose layouts are provided for events and fundraisers.

## Formatting Paragraphs

The appearance of your publications helps convey their message. By using the Publisher templates, you can develop professional-looking brochures whose appearance is appropriate to their contents. However, you can easily apply your own formatting to any part of a publication to get precisely the look you want.

As you know, all text in a publication is typed in a text box. You create *paragraphs* by typing text and pressing the Enter key. A paragraph can be a single word, a single sentence, or multiple sentences. You can change the look of the paragraph by clicking buttons on the Formatting toolbar.

Clicking the Line Spacing button displays the Paragraph dialog box, where you can adjust the space between lines within a paragraph and between paragraphs. You can also indent paragraphs from the left and right margins, as well as specify where the first line of a paragraph begins and where the second and subsequent lines begin in this dialog box. (To quickly indent entire paragraphs, you can click the indentation buttons on the toolbar.)

You can also determine the position of a paragraph between the left and right margins by changing its alignment. You can click the alignment buttons on the Formatting toolbar to align paragraphs as follows:

- Clicking the Align Text Left button aligns the left end of each line of the paragraph at the left margin, with a ragged right edge.

- Clicking the Align Text Right button aligns the right end of each line of the paragraph at the right margin, with a ragged left edge.

- Clicking the Center button aligns the center of each line of the paragraph between the left and right margins, with ragged left and right edges.

- Clicking the Justify button aligns the left and right ends of each line of the paragraph at the left and right margins, adjusting the space between words as necessary to achieve this.

Collectively, the settings you use to change the look of a paragraph are called *paragraph formatting*.

Setting a right indent indicates where all the lines in a paragraph should end, but sometimes you might want to specify where only one line should end. For example, you might want to break a title after a specific word to make it look balanced on the page. You can end an individual line at the insertion point without ending the paragraph by pressing Shift+Enter to insert a *line break*. You can see many types of line breaks and paragraph breaks (as well as spaces and tab marks) by selecting Special Characters on the View menu. The line break (line feed) character looks like a bent arrow, and the paragraph mark (¶) looks like a backward P. Inserting a line break does not start a new paragraph, so when you apply paragraph formatting to a line of text that ends with a line break, the formatting is applied to the entire paragraph.

> **Tip**  A paragraph's formatting is stored with its paragraph mark. If you delete the paragraph mark, thereby making the preceding text part of the following paragraph, that text takes on the formatting of the following paragraph. If you insert a paragraph break within a paragraph, the new paragraph takes on the formatting of the existing paragraph.

Every paragraph in a publication is formatted with a *style*, which is a collection of character and paragraph formatting. When you create a publication based on a template, the template's styles control the basic formatting of the publication and any changes you make to the character or paragraph formatting are applied on top of these styles. You can click a paragraph to see its style displayed in the Style box on the Formatting toolbar, and you can apply a different style by clicking it in the Style list. You can also display the Styles task pane and work with styles from there.

If the styles defined by a publication's template don't meet your needs, you can create your own styles in the following ways:

- By updating an existing style to reflect formatting you have manually applied to a paragraph
- By modifying an existing style in the Modify Style dialog box.
- By defining an existing combination of manually applied formatting as a style
- By creating the style manually in the New Style dialog box.

> **Tip**  Custom styles are available for use only in the publication in which you create them. You can import custom styles from an existing publication by clicking the Import Styles button in the Styles task pane. In the Import Styles dialog box, navigate to and double-click the publication containing the custom styles you want. Publisher then imports those styles into the current publication.

## Watermarks

There might be times when you want words or graphics to appear unobtrusively behind the text of a publication, usually in a pale font. For example, you might want the word *SALE* to appear behind the text in a promotional flyer, the word *DECEMBER* to appear behind the text in a menu, or your organization's logo to appear behind the text in a brochure. These faint background words and graphics are called *watermarks*. Watermarks are visible in a publication, but because they are faint, they don't interfere with the readers' ability to view the publication's main text.

To create a text watermark:

1. Insert a text box, size it to span the page, and then rotate it to the angle you want.

2. Type the text in the text box, select it, and on the **Formatting** toolbar, set the font and size so that the text fills the box.

3. On the **Formatting** toolbar, click the **Font Color** arrow, and then click **Fill Effects** to display the Fill Effects dialog box.

4. Set the **Base color** to the color you want. Then click one of the three lightest **Tint/Shade** boxes (10%, 20%, or 30%), and click **OK**.

To create a graphic watermark:

1. Insert and size the graphic as usual.

2. On the **Picture** toolbar, click the **Color** button, and then click **Washout**.

If you want to colorize the washed-out image you can do so on the Picture tab of the Format Picture dialog box. With Washout selected in the Color list, click Recolor, select the tint color you want, and then click OK.

If you want the watermark to appear on all the pages of a multi-page publication, add it to the publication's master page.

## Continuing Stories from One Text Box to Another

After you format the characters and paragraphs in a publication the way you want them, you can adjust the layout to accommodate the text. In a brochure that is designed to be folded, you might find that you need to continue text from a text box on one panel to a text box on a different panel. Publisher does not automatically flow text from box to box the way Word flows text from page to page. You have to explicitly link text boxes to tell Publisher where it should flow the text. This gives you control over the continuation of articles from page to page.

You create and break links and move between linked text boxes by clicking the buttons on the Connect Text Boxes toolbar.

### Multiple Columns

If you want to arrange text in two or more columns, it is not necessary to create multiple text boxes: You can format a text box to display its contents in columns.

To create columns, you click anywhere in the text box, click the Columns button on the Standard toolbar, and then click the number of columns you want (up to four). Publisher sets up the columns and flows the text from one to another automatically.

To fine-tune a multi-column layout, right-click a column, click Format Text Box, click the Text Box tab, and click Columns to display the Columns dialog box. You can then change the number of columns and adjust the spacing between them. In the Columns dialog box, you can divide a text box into a maximum of 63 columns. To draw a line between the columns, on the Colors And Lines tab of the Format Text Box dialog box, click the No Lines button under Presets, and then click the Center Vertical Line button in the Preview area. You can then specify a line color, choose dotted, dashed, double, or triple lines, and specify the line thickness.

## Flowing Text Around Objects

Because you need to entice a potential reader to open a brochure, most marketing materials of this type include eye-catching graphics on the wrapper. To arrange text and graphics in attractive layouts, you will often need to flow text around graphic objects in various ways. On the Layout tab of the Format Picture dialog box, you can choose from five different text-wrapping styles. If you choose a style that allows text to flow beside a graphic, you can wrap text on both sides, on one side, or in the largest space available. In addition, you can specify the spacing between the text and the graphic.

**Tip** You don't have to flow text around a graphic. On the Layout tab of the Format Picture dialog box, you can set the Object Position as Inline and select the Move Object With Text option to anchor the graphic to the text. Then if you add or delete text, the graphic moves with the text instead of the text moving around it.

To enable the Object Position option, the picture must be on top of the text box in the object stack.

In this exercise, you will create a brochure and then format its text manually and by customizing styles. You will link two text boxes to flow text from one to the other. Finally, you will change the text wrapping style of a photograph and balance the text in the text boxes on the inside page of the brochure.

**USE** the *Brochure* publication. This practice file is located in the *Documents\Microsoft Press\SBS_Publisher2007\MarketingMaterials* folder.

**BE SURE TO** close any open publications and display the Getting Started window before beginning this exercise.

1.  In the **Publication Types** list, click **Brochures**, and scroll the center pane to see the available templates.

    Each brochure design category is divided into purpose-specific brochure types.

2.  In the **Classic Designs** category, under **Informational**, click **Straight Edge**.

3.  Under **Customize** in the right pane, set the **Color scheme** to **Glacier** and the **Font scheme** to **Aspect**. (Keep the default settings under Options in the right pane.) Then click **Create**.

Open

4.  Take a look at the two pages of this brochure, and then on the **Standard** toolbar, click the **Open** button. In the **Open Publication** dialog box, navigate to the *Documents\Microsoft Press\SBS_Publisher2007\MarketingMaterials* folder, and double-click the *Brochure* publication.

    This is a customized version of the brochure you created. We have entered text, inserted graphics, and deleted extraneous elements so that you can focus on formatting the brochure.

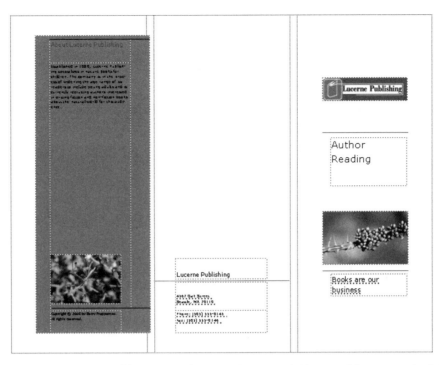

5. Close the Format Publication task pane. On page 1 (the outside wrapper) of the Author Reading brochure, click inside each text box in turn, noticing the style name that appears in the **Style** box on the **Formatting** toolbar. Then display page 2, and click inside each of its text boxes.

   Paragraphs of the same style look the same, no matter where they appear in the brochure.

6. Display page 1. In the right section of the page, select **Author Reading** (click it and press Ctrl + A, or drag across it), and then on the **Formatting** toolbar, do the following:

   ● Click the **Bold** button.

   ● Click the **Font Size** arrow, and then in the list, click **26**.

   ● Click the **Align Text Right** button.

7. Select **Books are our business**, make it bold, and then right-align it.

8. In the middle section of the page, select **Lucerne Publishing**, increase its size to **16** points, and then change its color to purple (**Followed Hyperlink**).

9. In the left section of the page, click **About Lucerne Publishing**, and change the **Zoom** level to **100%**. Then click to the left of **Lucerne**, and press ⌈Shift⌉ + ⌈Enter⌉ to insert a line break. Select all the text in the text box, increase the font size to **12** points, and make the text bold. Finally, change the **Zoom** level to **Whole Page**.

10. Select all the text in the box below **About Lucerne Publishing**, and increase its size to **14** points. Then click a blank area of the page to see the results.

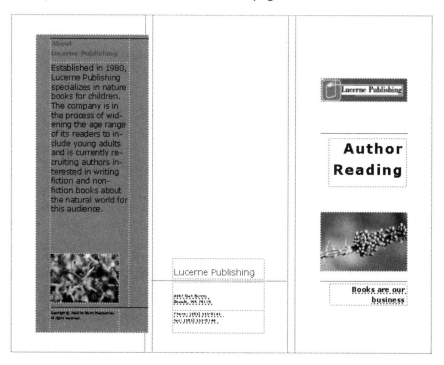

The paragraph you just formatted is styled as Normal, which is also applied to paragraphs on page 2 of the brochure. Let's change the Normal style so that the text in the Normal paragraphs on page 2 automatically appears at the same size as in this one.

**11.** Select the paragraph again. Then on the **Format** menu, click **Styles** to display the **Styles** task pane.

**12.** In the task pane, point to **Normal**, click the arrow that appears, and then click **Update to match selection**.

The look of Normal changes in the task pane to reflect the formatting applied to the paragraph.

**13.** Display page 2 to verify that the font size of its Normal paragraphs has changed to reflect the modified style.

**14.** In the left section of the page, click anywhere in the text box containing **JUST PUBLISHED**, scroll the styles list in the **Styles** task pane, and click **Title 2**. Then select the title, make it bold, and change its color to teal (**Accent 1**).

**15.** Click the text box below the title.

The Text In Overflow button appears below the text box, indicating that this box contains more text than is displayed.

Create Text
Box Link

**16.** On the **Connect Text Boxes** toolbar, click the **Create Text Box Link** button. Move the pointer over the empty text box in the middle section of the page, and when the pointer changes to a pouring pitcher, click the mouse button.

> **Troubleshooting** You can flow text only into an empty text box. When pointing to a text box that contains content, the pointer resembles an upright pitcher and the linking function is disabled.

Publisher flows the additional text into the linked text box.

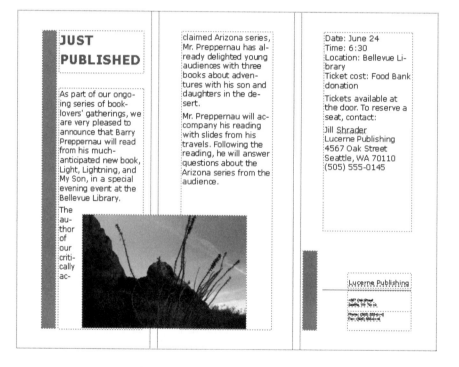

> **Tip** To unlink two text boxes, click the first box and then on the Connect Text Boxes toolbar, click the Break Forward Link button.

You don't want the text in the first text box to dribble down the left side of the photograph at the bottom of the brochure, so you need to adjust the way Publisher flows text around the photograph.

Format Picture

**17.** Click the photograph, and then on the **Picture** toolbar, click the **Format Picture** button. In the **Format Picture** dialog box, click the **Layout** tab.

**Format Picture**

Tabs: Colors and Lines | Size | Layout | Picture | Text Box | Web

Object Position: Exact

Position on page

Horizontal: 1.75"  From: Top Left Corner
Vertical: 5.125"  From: Top Left Corner

Wrapping Style

Square | Tight | Through | Top and bottom | None

Wrap text
◉ Both sides  ◯ Left only  ◯ Right only  ◯ In largest space available

Distance from text
☑ Automatic   Top 0.04"   Left 0.04"
              Bottom 0.04"   Right 0.04"

OK | Cancel | Help

**18.** Under **Wrapping Style**, click **Top and Bottom**, and then click **OK**.

Publisher moves the text from the left side of the photograph to the top of the text box on the second panel. Now let's fine-tune the layout to balance the text in the three panels.

**19.** On the **Arrange** menu, point to **Ruler Guides**, and click **Add Horizontal Ruler Guide**. Then drag the guide down until it is approximately aligned with the last line of text in the center text box.

**20.** Click the border of the left text box, and then press the ↑ key repeatedly until the last line in the text box is aligned with the ruler guide.

**21.** Click after the word **donation** in the right text box, and press Enter. Then click after the word **contact**, and press Enter.

**22.** Scrutinize the words that Publisher has automatically hyphenated, and if you want, insert line breaks to override the hyphenation.

For example, we inserted a line break to the left of the word *Library* in the right panel.

**See Also** For information about hyphenation, see "Controlling Hyphenation" in Chapter 5, "Creating Text-Based Publications."

**23.** Click a blank area of the brochure. Then on the **View** menu, click **Boundaries and Guides** to turn off the guides and see the results.

You can now print two-sided copies of the brochure, fold them in three, and distribute them.

**CLOSE** the open publications without saving your changes, and if you are not continuing on to the next chapter, quit Publisher.

# Key Points

- Whether you are creating publications for an individual, a group, a company, or an organization, developing a consistent look for all communications helps to build an identity, or brand.

- When a brand builds goodwill and trust, it becomes a valuable asset. If that asset is a name, graphic image, or slogan, you might want to claim ownership by registering it as a trademark or service mark.

- A well-designed publication relies on a balanced layout that is easier to achieve if you work with an underlying grid.

- Formatting a publication can be as simple as changing the font scheme or as complex as changing individual formatting attributes such as font, size, effect, color, alignment, and spacing.

- You can apply combinations of formatting with a couple of clicks by defining and using styles.

# Chapter at a Glance

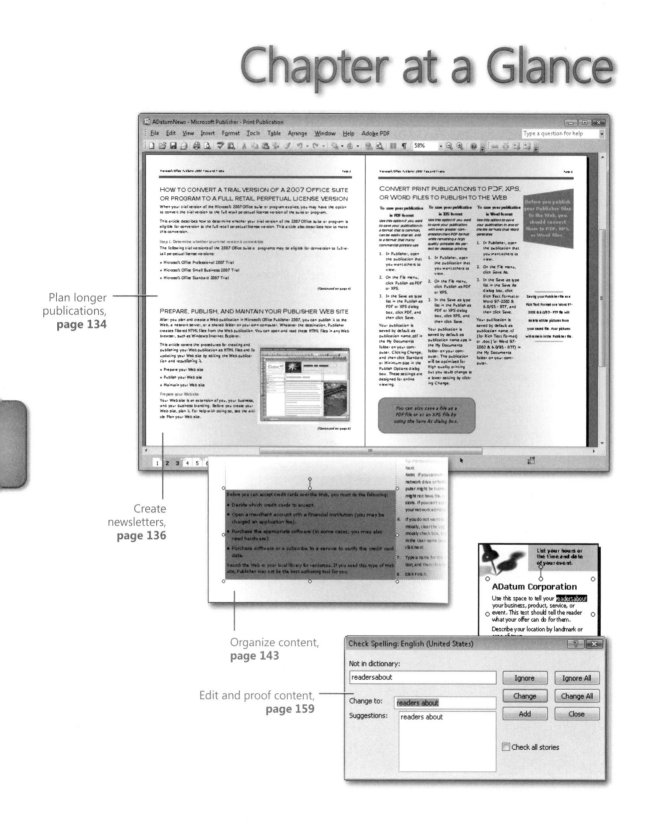

Plan longer publications,
**page 134**

Create newsletters,
**page 136**

Organize content,
**page 143**

Edit and proof content,
**page 159**

# 5 Creating Text-Based Publications

---

**In this chapter, you will learn to:**

- ✔ Plan longer publications.
- ✔ Create newsletters.
- ✔ Organize content.
- ✔ Edit and proof content.

---

Most publications contain text, even if it is just a heading or two. However, some types of publications rely mostly on text to convey information, with graphics and other elements playing only a supporting role. Text-based publications that are more than a couple of pages in length, especially those containing multiple stories, pose unique challenges, such as how to flow text logically across multiple pages, how to juggle pages containing differ- ent kinds of content, and how to efficiently edit the text and ensure that it is error-free.

In this chapter, you will first review design concepts that pertain to longer publications. Then you will create a multi-page newsletter; size text to fit the available space, and add pages. You will continue stories by linking and unlinking text boxes, insert and remove Continued notices, move and delete pages, and format text in columns. Finally, you will edit a publication in Microsoft Office Word and correct its spelling in Microsoft Office Publisher 2007.

**See Also** Do you need only a quick refresher on the topics in this chapter? See the Quick Reference entries on pages xxvii–xli.

> **Important** Before you can use the practice files in this chapter, you need to install them from the book's companion CD to their default location. See "Using the Book's CD" on page xvii for more information.

> **Troubleshooting**  Graphics and operating system–related instructions in this book reflect the Windows Vista user interface. If your computer is running Windows XP and you experience trouble following the instructions as written, please refer to the "Information for Readers Running Windows XP" section at the beginning of this book.

# Planning Longer Publications

Most of the publications we've created in this book have been from one to four pages long, which is the length specified by most Publisher design and layout templates. However, you can create longer publications, either by inserting pages in a template-based publication or by creating a publication from scratch. You can create an 8-page menu, a 12-page newsletter, a 100-page report, a 1000-page book—the possibilities are limited only by your imagination and by printing practicalities.

When producing a publication that will contain a lot of content, you can save time by planning its design before you start creating it. Many of the decisions you will need to make for printed publications are based on the quantity you need to produce, the quality you want to achieve, and the amount of money you want to invest. For a printed publication, you will need to consider the following:

- **Color.**  Will the printed publication be four-color (photographic quality), two-color (usually black plus an accent color), or monochromatic? Color is more expensive, regardless of the production method.

- **Physical size and format.**  Approximately how many pages will the publication include? Will the format fit a standard paper size or require trimming? Do you plan to distribute the publication in a stapled, full-page format; in a loose-leaf ring binder; as a folded and stapled booklet; or as a bound document? Some binding methods can support up to a maximum number of pages; if you produce a 1000-page training manual, for example, stapling and tape binding are not viable options.

- **Production method.**  How many copies of the publication will you produce? Will you print only one copy of the publication for reproduction, or one copy for each recipient? Will you print the publication on your own printer, at a copy shop, or through a professional printing service?

Other design considerations apply to all types of publications, whether intended for printing or for electronic distribution. For any publication, you will need to consider the following:

- **Basic layout.** Where will you start your publication design? Can you use an existing Publisher template? If you will create similar publications in the future, do you need to design a custom template? For a custom template, will it be easier to start with a Publisher design or layout template and then add and remove elements as necessary? Or should you start from a blank page, insert the specific design elements you need, and then save the publication as a template?

> **Important** You don't have to create a template for a one-time publication. However, saving the publication as a template makes it available for use in the event that you create a second publication of the same type or of a similar type. It also makes it easier to start over if you encounter a problem with your first attempt.

- **Text design.** Can you use an existing font scheme and color scheme? Or do you need to create custom schemes? The font and font size you select can have a significant impact on the length of your publication.

  **See Also** For more information about the impact of fonts on publication length, see "Solving Organization Problems," later in this chapter.

- **Page types.** Will your publication include multiple page types, such as a cover page, a page for contributions from regular columnists or readers, an order form, and so on? If this is a periodic publication, you will want to place repeating features such as a letter from the editor or a contact list in the same location in each issue so that readers know where to find it.

- **Static information.** Will each issue of a periodic publication include static information, such as the title, return address, and logo, in the same places? You can save time by entering that information before saving the publication as a template.

If you do need to create a custom design, page layouts, a font scheme, or a color scheme, do this first so that when you flow content into the publication, it immediately appears in its final format. By laying the groundwork, you can quickly identify and handle content issues as they arise.

> **Tip** To save a publication as a template, click Save As on the File menu, and then in the Save As Type list, click Publisher Template. Publisher saves all the content along with the design, layout, font scheme, and color scheme.

### Non-Standard Sizes

Publisher comes with templates for a wide variety of publications. Most are appropriate for use by businesses and community organizations, many are useful for personal or family occasions, and a few are just for fun. Among the latter are the paper-folding templates from which you can create paper airplanes or origami models. (The airplane templates even include optional aerodynamic indicators.)

Most of the templates we work with in this book are designed for printing on standard-sized paper, but Publisher also provides for the non-standard publications you might need to complete your branding portfolio. You can create large items, such as banners and signs, and small items, such as advertisements and gift certificates, using the same resources and techniques you would for any other publication. Although these publications are not primarily text-based, they can present copyfitting challenges that you will be better equipped to meet after reading this chapter.

# Creating Newsletters

A *newsletter* is a periodic publication containing information of interest to a specific group—for example, employees of a company or members of a club or other organization. Newsletter recipients are frequently subscribers you track in a mailing list, rather than people you don't know. Depending on the size of your subscription base and the amount and frequency of information in each newsletter, you might choose to deliver the content in a traditional printed format or in an electronic format, such as on a Web site or by e-mail.

**See Also**  For information about electronic publications, see Chapter 6, "Communicating Your Message Online."

Publisher 2007 includes over 60 preformatted newsletter designs. When creating a newsletter based on one of these templates, you can choose a one-page spread, appropriate for printing on separate sheets of paper, or a two-page spread, appropriate for a booklet-style publication. If you will distribute the newsletter by mail, you can designate a portion of the back page for mailing information. This area, which is designed to be visible when you fold the publication, includes areas for information about your organization, postage, and recipient details. To enter the recipient details, you can hand-write names and addresses, affix mailing labels, or merge the newsletter with a recipient list to create an individual publication for each recipient.

**See Also**  For information about merging publications with a data source, see "Using Mail Merge" in Chapter 3, "Creating Colorful Cards and Calendars."

## Copyfitting Text

When you customize the placeholder text in a newsletter that is based on a Publisher template, you will often find that your text does not fit the ready-made text boxes as neatly as the placeholder text did. When this happens, you can change the size of the text box, manually format the text to make it fit, or have Publisher automatically *copyfit* the text.

When you insert more text in a text box than can fit, one of the following three things happens:

● If the text box is linked to another text box, the remaining text flows into the next text box.

● If the text box is not linked to another text box and automatic copyfitting is turned off, the Text In Overflow icon appears, and the text size does not change.

● If the text box is not linked to another text box and automatic copyfitting is turned on, the text size decreases until the text fits.

Copyfitting is turned on by default for some text boxes created as part of a Publisher design or layout template, such as those intended for headings. Copyfitting is turned off for general-use text boxes and those that you insert manually. You can turn copyfitting on or off for a selected text box by clicking an AutoFit Text option on the Format menu or by clicking the Text Autofitting option you want on the Text Box tab of the Format Text Box dialog box.

## Inserting Pages

Newsletters are generally text-based but frequently contain other types of information. Publisher provides five standard newsletter page layouts: Story, Calendar, Order Form, Response Form, and Sign-Up Form. You can also insert a specified number of blank pages before or after the current page, or you can duplicate an existing page layout a specified number of times. (This option is particularly handy if you create your own page layouts.)

In this exercise, you will create a newsletter with a color scheme appropriate for photo-copying. You will replace placeholder text, copyfit the text to the text boxes in which it appears, and add pages to accommodate the intended newsletter content. There is no practice file for this exercise.

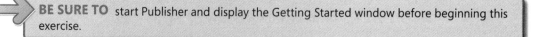

**BE SURE TO** start Publisher and display the Getting Started window before beginning this exercise.

1. In the **Publication Types** list, click **Newsletters**.

2. Scroll the list in the center pane to see the available newsletter templates. Then in the **Classic Designs** category, click **Banded**.

3. Under **Customize** in the right pane, set the **Color scheme** to **Black & Gray** and the **Font scheme** to **Virtual**.

4. Under **Options**, set the **Page size** to **One-page spread**, and select the **Include customer address** check box. Then click **Create**.

   Publisher creates a four-page newsletter with all design elements, other than placeholder graphics, rendered in shades of black and gray.

5. Close the **Format Publication** task pane, and then set the **Zoom** level to **Page Width**.

   The organization name from the active information set appears in the upper-left corner of this front page. Generic placeholders indicate where to insert the newsletter title and edition-specific information.

6. Click **Newsletter Title**, and type Technology Times. Click **Newsletter Date**, and type April 1, 2008. Then click **Volume 1, Issue 1**, and type Technical support at your fingertips!

   **Troubleshooting** As you type the word *your*, the text disappears. Keep typing, even though you can't see the result.

Publisher displays the Text In Overflow indicator to signal that more text is in the selected text box than is shown.

Text In Overflow indicator

7. On the **Format** menu, point to **AutoFit Text**, and then click **Shrink Text On Overflow**.

   Publisher shrinks the text so that the entire slogan is now visible. However, it is very small.

8. Drag the right handle of the text box to the right until the text box overlaps the text box containing the date. Release the mouse button when the right edge of the selected text box is slightly to the left of the word *April*. Then click away from the box to see the results.

9. On the page sorter, click the **Page 2** button to display page 2. Then scroll the page to view the placeholder content.

   Placeholder stories within each set of linked text boxes provide useful information about newsletter design and content. The newsletter title you entered in step 7 appears in a text box at the bottom of the page.

10. Display page 3, and scroll to the top of the page.

   The slogan you entered in step 6 is only partially visible in the text box in the upper-left corner of the page, because the text box is not wide enough to accommodate it.

11. Click the text box that contains the slogan, and drag the right handle to the right so that the text box fills the available space to the left of the text box containing the page number. Then on the **Format** menu, point to **AutoFit Text**, and click **Best Fit**.

   The font size of the slogan text increases to fit the wider text box.

   At the beginning of each story is the approximate number of words that fits in the set of linked text boxes. This estimate is based on the default font scheme for this template, which you changed before creating the publication.

12. Click anywhere in the first story on page 3.

   Publisher selects the first text box in the story and displays the Go To Next Text Box button.

Go to Next
Text Box

13. Click the **Go to Next Text Box** button.

   Publisher selects the last text box in the story and displays the Go To Previous Text Box button and the Text In Overflow indicator. At the current font size, the place-holder text for this story does not fit in the space provided.

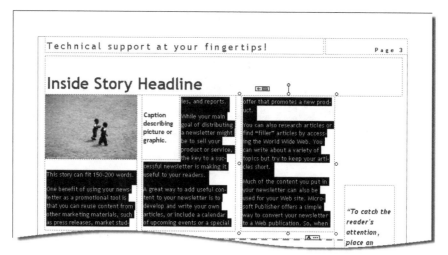

This newsletter will contain several lengthy stories, so you need to add pages to accommodate them.

**14.** On the **Insert** menu, click **Duplicate Page**.

Publisher inserts a new page 4 with the same layout as page 3.

**15.** On the **Insert** menu, click **Page**.

The Insert Newsletter Page dialog box opens.

**16.** Click the **Available page types** arrow to display the types of pages you can insert.

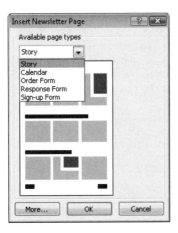

**17.** Click each type in turn to display a preview of the page layout.

Each page type includes at least one story area, giving you many options.

**18.** In the **Available page types** list, click **Story**. Then click **More**.

The Insert Page dialog box opens.

From this dialog box, you can insert multiple pages containing no design elements, one text box, or the same layout as the currently selected page.

**19.** In the **Number of new pages** box, enter 3, and in the **Options** area, click **Duplicate all objects on page**. Then click **OK**.

Publisher inserts three more identical pages.

**20.** Display page 7. On the **Insert** menu, click **Page**. In the **Insert Newsletter Page** dialog box, click **Calendar** in the **Available page types** list, and then click **OK**.

Publisher inserts a page containing a calendar with a schedule of events, space for one story, and one graphic with a caption. The Zoom level changes to display the whole page.

> **Troubleshooting**  The new calendar page uses a different font scheme than the one you selected when you created the newsletter. In fact, the font scheme for the entire publication has reverted back to the default for the template on which it is based to maintain consistency with the newly inserted page. Refer to step 22 for more information.

**21.** Repeat step 20 to insert an **Order Form**, a **Response Form**, and a **Sign-up Form**.

The resulting publication includes 12 pages.

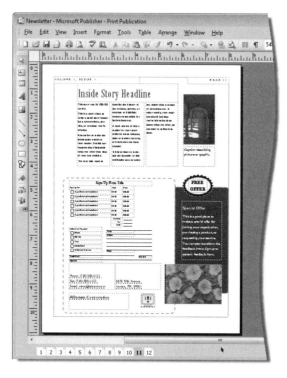

22. Display the **Font Schemes** section of the **Format Publication** task pane.

    The Virtual font scheme appears to be selected, but in fact the publication has reverted to the default font scheme for the Banded newsletter template, which is at the top of the list.

23. In the font scheme list, click **Virtual** to reapply the font scheme to the publication.

24. Display page 12 to view the customer information section and other outside page content.

**CLOSE** the publication without saving your changes.

# Organizing Content

Longer publications often include several independent stories that compete for the reader's attention. Before entering content into a newsletter or other long publication, it is wise to decide where to place each piece of content within the overall context of the publication. For example, in a newsletter, important stories should start on the first page but can continue inside the publication, most likely near the end. Some people think that stories that start on the right page of a two-page spread are more likely to be read than stories that start on the left page. In a publication that will be folded for mailing, place information that you definitely want the recipient to see on the first or last (outside) page.

## Working with a Table of Contents

A longer publication can often benefit from a navigational aid such as a table of contents. When you create a publication such as a newsletter, Publisher inserts a table of contents object on the first page of the publication. You must then manually customize the object to reflect the publication's contents.

You can insert a table of contents object anywhere in a publication from the Design Gallery. You can choose from 34 designs, each color-coordinated with the current publication font scheme. If you know the name of the design or layout template the publication is based on, you might find a coordinating table of contents object.

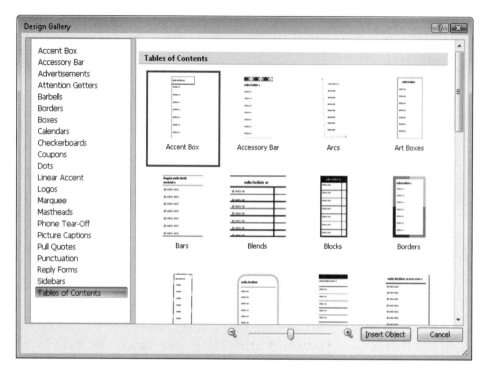

**See Also**  For information about inserting objects from the Design Gallery, see "Working with Pre-Designed Visual Elements" in Chapter 2, "Creating Visual Interest."

> **Troubleshooting**  After inserting a table of contents object, you can't change its design. However, changes you make to the publication font scheme or color scheme are applied to the table of contents object.

Each table of contents object includes graphic elements and a table containing place-holders for a header, article names, and page numbers. You must manually replace the text with your own. If you move information or add pages, Publisher will not automatically update the page number in the table of contents, so it's a good idea to insert the information in the table of contents after you finalize the page layout.

To change the layout of a table of contents object—for example, to add or remove rows—right-click the table part of the object, click Format Table, and then format it as you would any other table.

**See Also**  For information about working with tables, see the sidebar titled "Presenting Information in Tables and Lists" in Chapter 6, "Communicating Your Message Online."

# Creating Sections

If the topics in a long publication fall logically into groups—for example, parts, subjects, or time periods—you can formally title these groups by assigning them to *sections*. You can then include only the sections—preceded by any *front matter* (such as an introduction) and followed by any *back matter* (such as a list of resources or a bibliography)—in the primary table of contents at the beginning of the publication, and include a list of topics in a secondary table of contents at the beginning of each section.

> **Tip** You can insert another type of section break within a paragraph to cause its text to continue in the next linked text box. To insert a paragraph section break, press Ctrl+Enter.

To create a section, select the page that you want to designate as its beginning. (If your publication has two-page spreads, begin each section on a right page—called a *recto* page in the publishing world; the left page is called a *verso* page—so that the section title falls on the front side of the leaf and faces the reader.) Then click Section on the Insert menu. In the Section dialog box, select the Begin A Section With This Page check box, and then indicate whether you want the page to display headers and footers, and whether to restart the page numbering or continue from the previous section. You can choose from a variety of page-numbering formats and designate the beginning page number.

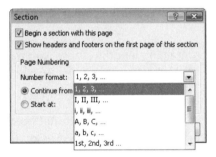

> **Tip** You cannot automatically include the section number as part of the page-numbering format. As a workaround, you can manually insert it in the text box containing the page number.

In some types of publications, such as reports, you might want to draw attention to the starting point of each section by designing a special page called a *section opener*. If the last page of the previous section ends on a recto, you can insert a blank verso page to force the section opener onto a recto. If you use openers, you will want to clear the

Show Headers And Footers On the First Page Of This Section check box before clicking OK to close the Section dialog box. (You will need to manually remove the header and footer from a preceding blank page.)

> **Tip** On the page sorter, a space appears between sections.

## Moving Content

In Chapter 4, "Marketing Your Product, Service, or Organization," we briefly discussed flowing information that doesn't fit in one text box into another; this is called *continuing a story*. In many types of publications, each story appears on one page, whether as a full page of text, multiple columns within a text box, or multiple text boxes organized to fit the space. In some types of publications, however, you might need to continue a story elsewhere in the publication.

For example, in a newspaper the first few paragraphs of the most important story usually appear on the front page of the main section, while the first few paragraphs of a less important story might begin on the next spread. The remainder of each article appears further back. In a magazine, the first few pages of a long article might appear in one place and the final pages might be relegated to the back of the magazine. In Publisher layout terms, the stories would flow through one or more text boxes on one page to text boxes on later pages.

During the review process of a publication containing lengthy stories, you might find that due to changes, additions, or deletions, you need to change the flow of a story. You can move the text boxes and pages containing content in the following ways:

- To move a text box elsewhere on the same page, point to its outer border, and then when the pointer changes to a four-headed arrow, drag it to its new location.
- To move a text box to a location on another page, do one of these two things:
    - Drag the text box into the scratch area, display the destination page, and then drag the text box to the desired location.
    - Cut the text box to the Clipboard, display the destination page, paste the text box (it appears either on the page or in the scratch area) and then drag it to the desired location.
- To move a page to another location, drag the page icon in the page sorter. As you drag, a black arrow indicates the insertion location. Release the mouse button when the page is where you want it.

> **Troubleshooting** When you move a text box, its content moves with it, and it retains any links to other text boxes. Moving a linked text box or a page containing linked text boxes could result in segments of a story appearing out of order.

## Graphics Manager

In a multi-page publication that includes graphics, you can quickly view, locate, or replace graphics by using the Graphics Manager task pane. This task pane displays the file name and page number of all embedded or linked graphics in the publication, plus either the file size or a thumbnail of each graphic.

You can sort the graphics list by file name, file extension, file size, page number, and status (embedded or linked). If you work with linked graphics, the Graphics Manager task pane identifies any missing or modified images that need your attention.

To display the Graphics Manager task pane, click Graphics Manager on the Tools menu or in the task pane header list.

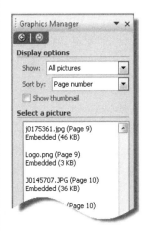

When you point to a graphic in the Select A Picture list, a ScreenTip displays the file name, file extension, file size, page number, and status of the graphic, and an arrow appears. Clicking the arrow displays a menu from which you can move to and select the image, convert an embedded image to a linked image or vice versa, replace the image, or display additional image properties including scaling, resolution, and color model.

## Solving Organization Problems

When you flow a story into one or more text boxes, the story might be too long or too short to conform to the allocated space. To address this type of problem, you can take one or more of the following actions:

- **Add or remove text.** If you have editorial control over the content, you can add or remove a word, sentence, or paragraph to fit the available space. Removing text is not necessarily a bad thing; just remember Mark Twain's famous quote, "If I had more time, I'd have written a shorter book."

- **Add, remove, or resize graphics.** A picture might not be worth 1000 words, but it can easily be made to occupy the space of 20, 50, or 100 words.

- **Add, remove, or link to text boxes.** Continue a long story into an additional text box on the same page or on another page. If a story does not require all the linked text boxes associated with it, you must manually break the forward links from the last occupied text box to the subsequent linked text boxes in the set.

> **Tip** To cleanly disconnect multiple unused linked text boxes, move to the final linked text box in the set by pressing the Go To Next Text Box button at the bottom of each text box. From the final text box, press the Go To Previous Text Box button. Then on the Connect Text Boxes toolbar, click the Break Forward Link button. Continue this process until the last occupied text box is the final box in the set.

- **Resize text boxes.** This isn't quite as simple a solution as it might sound. To make one text box taller, shorter, wider, or narrower, you will probably have to resize others, either to make space, fill space, or balance the design.

  To change the height of a set of identically sized text boxes simultaneously, select the first text box, press and hold the Shift key, and select the other text boxes. (The Group button will appear.) Then drag the top or bottom handle of any one of the selected text boxes to resize them all.

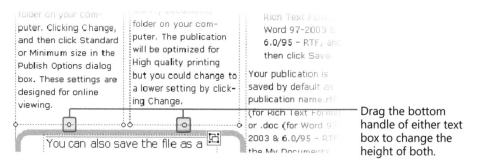

Drag the bottom handle of either text box to change the height of both.

● **Change the layout of text within the text box or within the story.** You can change the amount of white space that appears around the text in a text box (increasing the margin decreases the text area), change the number of columns within a text box, or change the number of text boxes that contain the story. For example, changing from three narrow columns of justified paragraphs to two wider columns can be enough to shorten the content by a line or two.

> **Tip** You can change the margins of a single text box from the Text Box tab of the Format Text Box dialog box. To automatically apply the modified text box settings to all new text boxes added to the publication, select the Apply Settings To New Text Boxes check box on the Colors And Lines tab.

● **Change the font or font size of the story.** If your design uses multiple fonts or sizes, you can apply one of the other available fonts or sizes to the story in a text box. However, changing to a font or size that is not used anywhere else in the publication can be distracting and look amateurish.

> **Tip** You might be tempted to change the margins of a publication to try to change its *footprint*. You can relocate the blue margin guides by clicking Layout Guides on the Arrange menu and entering new top, bottom, left, and right margins on the Margin Guides tab. However, the layout of your publication does not change to reflect the new margin settings, so this adjustment essentially has no effect on the footprint.

In shorter publications such as flyers and tri-fold brochures, it is reasonably simple to rearrange text boxes and resize content to appropriately fill the available space. Longer publications present additional challenges: You might need to conform to a 16-page *signature* for an offset-printed publication, to a 4-page footprint for each *leaf* added to a folded publication, or to a 2-page footprint for each leaf of a loose leaf, double-sided publication. After you insert all the content you intend to use in a publication and adjust the size of each story's text boxes to fit its content, you might find that the publication is too long or too short to fit the intended footprint. You might be able to fix the problem by adding, removing, or changing individual stories, but if that is not possible, you can also solve the problem by making global changes to the publication.

One way to manage the length of your publication is through your choice of font scheme. Different fonts have different height-to-width relationships—for example, the letter *m* is narrower in 12-point Calibri than it is in 12-point Verdana. The difference may be slight on a letter-by-letter basis, but it can be significant when applied to an entire publication.

**The quick brown fox jumps over the lazy dog.**

The quick brown fox jumps over the lazy dog.

The quick brown fox jumps over the lazy dog.

**The quick brown fox jumps over the lazy dog.**

The quick brown fox jumps over the lazy dog.

**The quick brown fox jumps over the lazy dog.**

The quick brown fox jumps over the lazy dog.

The Font Scheme list, both in the Getting Started window and in the Format Publication task pane, displays three pieces of information for each font scheme: the scheme name, the primary font, and the secondary font. The primary font is used for headings and titles, and the secondary font for body text. The names of the primary and secondary fonts are displayed in those fonts, providing a means by which you can gauge the effect each scheme will have on the length of your publication.

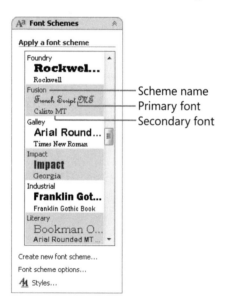

Scheme name
Primary font
Secondary font

**Tip** You cannot make changes to the font schemes that come with Publisher, but you can create a custom font scheme, either from scratch or based on an existing scheme. You can change, rename, and delete custom font schemes.

In this exercise, you will trace the continuation of a story; move, insert, and delete pages; insert and remove Continued notices; format text in columns; and connect and disconnect text boxes.

> **USE** the *ADatumNews* publication. This practice file is located in the *Documents\Microsoft Press\SBS_Publisher2007\TextPublications* folder.
>
> **OPEN** the *ADatumNews* publication, and close the Format Publication task pane.

1. If you have a printer available, print the publication (double-sided, if possible) to make it easier to follow along with the exercise.

2. On the **View** menu, select **Two-Page Spread** if it is not already selected. Then on the page sorter, click the **Page 2** button to display pages 2 and 3.

   The publication contains five stories: Two start on page 1 and continue later in the publication, two start on page 2 and continue later in the publication, and one complete story appears on page 3.

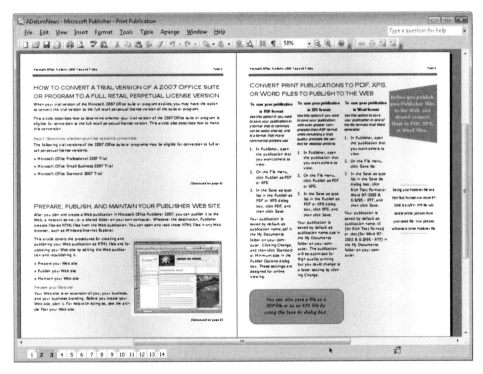

3. On the page sorter, do the following:

   ● Click the **Page 4** button to display pages 4 and 5.

   The first story beginning on page 2 continues on page 4 and ends halfway through page 5; the other half of the two-column text box on page 5 is empty.

> **Tip** You can follow the stories by clicking the Go To Previous Text Box and Go To Next Text Box buttons.

● Display pages 6 and 7, then 8 and 9, and then 10 and 11.

The second story beginning on page 2 continues on page 6 and runs through to page 10, ending partway down the left text box.

The second story beginning on page 1 continues in the right text box on page 10, runs through page 11, and ends near the top of the left text box on page 12.

● Display pages 12 and 13, and then click anywhere in the large text box on page 13.

On page 12, most of the left text box is empty, and the right text box is entirely empty. A sidebar relating to the story that ends at the top of the page spans the bottom of the page.

The first story beginning on page 1 continues on page 13. The Text In Overflow icon at the bottom of the page indicates that the story includes additional content that can't be shown in the allocated space.

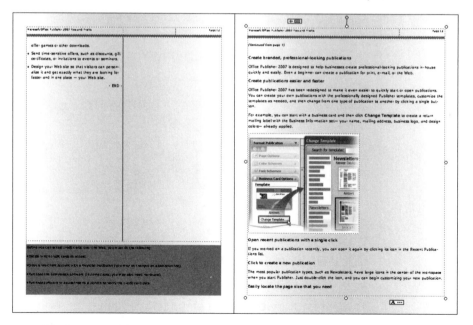

● Display page 14.

The last page of the publication is self-contained and complete.

You need to reorganize the publication so that the stories continue in the order in which they begin.

Go to Next
Text Box

**4.** Return to page 1. Click in the text box containing the story titled *What's New in Publisher 2007?*, and then click the **Go to Next Text Box** button that appears below the text box.

Publisher moves to page 13. The story does not connect to additional text boxes, so you need to move only this page to follow page 3.

**5.** On the **View** menu, click **Two-Page Spread** to turn off that view.

> **Tip** In Two-Page Spread view, moving either page of a spread on the page sorter moves both pages.

**6.** On the page sorter, drag page 13 after page 3, so that it becomes page 4.

You need to accommodate the part of the story that is not visible.

**7.** Click in the text box. On the **Format** menu, click **Text Box**, and then in the **Format Text Box** dialog box, display the **Text Box** tab.

> **Tip** The two Include "Continued" check boxes govern whether previous and next page numbers appear at the beginning and/or end of the selected text box. By default, you must manually select these check boxes for each text box in which you want the *Continued* text to appear. If you want one or both of these elements to appear by default, you can set your preferences here and then on the Colors And Lines tab, select the Apply Settings To New Text Boxes check box.

8. Clear the **Include "Continued on page..."** check box. Then click the **Columns** button.

   The Columns dialog box opens.

9. Change **Number** to 2, click **OK**, and then click **OK** in the **Format Text Box** dialog box.

   The text box contents flow into two columns, leaving considerable empty space at the bottom of the right column. However, the Text In Overflow icon indicates that additional text exists.

10. In the left column, click the picture. Then drag its lower-right handle up and to the left until the right edge of the picture aligns with the right edge of the column.

   When you release the handle, additional text and a graphic appear in the right column.

11. Repeat step 10 to resize the graphic in the right column to fit the column. Then click in the text box.

    The Text In Overflow icon still appears.

12. On the **Insert** menu, click **Duplicate Page** to insert a new page 5 containing an empty two-column text box.

Create Text
Box Link

13. Display page 4, click in the text box, and then on the **Connect Text Boxes** toolbar, click the **Create Text Box Link** button.

    When you move the pointer back over the publication window, it changes to a pitcher.

14. Display page 5, and click in the text box.

    Additional content fills page 5. The Text In Overflow Icon still appears.

15. Right-click the text box, click **Format Text Box**, and then click the **Text Box** tab. Clear the **Include "Continued from page..."** check box, and then click **OK**.

    It is unnecessary to include continuation messages when a story appears on consecutive pages.

16. On the **Insert** menu, click **Page**, and in the **Insert Newsletter Pages** dialog box, click **More**.

    The Insert Page dialog box opens.

17. Set the **Number of new pages** to 3, click the **Duplicate all objects on page** option, and then click **OK**.

    Publisher inserts four new pages (6, 7, and 8) containing empty two-column text boxes. The publication now has 18 pages.

18. Display page 5, and click in the text box. Click the **Create Text Box Link** button, display page 6, and click in the text box to continue the story. Repeat the process two times to continue the story through to page 8. Then resize each graphic to the width of its column.

    The story ends partway down the left column on page 8.

19. Click the text box, and then drag the bottom handle up to halfway through the content, releasing the mouse button when the content fills the two-column text box.

Microsoft Office Publisher 2007 Tips and Tricks | Page 8

tent across the 2007 Microsoft Office system programs. Examples of this change include:

- Several spelling checker options are now global. If you change one of these options in one Office program, that option is also changed for all the other Office programs. For more information, see Change the way spelling and grammar checking work.

- In addition to sharing the same custom dictionaries, all programs can manage them using the same dialog box. For more information, see Use custom dictionaries to add words to the spelling checker.

- The 2007 Microsoft Office system spelling checker includes the post-reform French dictionary. In Microsoft Office 2003, this was an add-in that had to be separately installed.

- An exclusion dictionary is automatically created for a language the first time that language is used. Exclusion dictionaries let you force the spelling checker flag words you want to avoid using. They are handy for avoiding words that are obscene or that don't match your style guide. For more information, see Use exclusion dictionaries to specify a preferred spelling for a word.

**Diagnose computer problems**

Microsoft Office Diagnostics is a series of diagnostic tests that can help you to discover why your computer is crashing. The diagnostic tests can solve some problems directly and may identify ways that you can solve other problems. Microsoft Office Diagnostics replaces the following Microsoft Office 2003 features: Detect and Repair and Microsoft Office Application Recovery.

---

**Troubleshooting** Be sure to size the window as shown in this graphic, or later steps might not work as expected.

---

**20.** Insert a copy of the text box at the bottom of the page, and size it to completely fill the available space. Using the skills you have learned, format the text box to include the "Continued from page" message when it contains text.

You will continue the second story from page 1 in this text box.

**21.** Display page 1, click in the text box containing the story titled *Plan Your Web Site*, and then click the **Go to Next Text Box** button that appears.

Publisher moves to the second column on page 15.

Break Forward
Link

**22.** Return to the previous text box, and on the **Connect Text Boxes** toolbar, click the **Break Forward Link** button.

The Text In Overflow icon appears. On pages 15 through 17, the text boxes that previously held the continued story are now empty.

**23.** Move page 16, which now contains an empty two-column text box, to become page 9. Then use the skills you have learned to continue the second story that begins on page 1 (*Plan Your Web Site*) in the lower text box on page 8 and then in the text box on page 9.

**24.** Click the **Go to Next Text Box** button at the bottom of page 9.

Publisher moves to page 17, where the only content in the text box is the indicator of the end of the story (- END -).

> **Troubleshooting**  If your page 17 contains additional content, the likelihood is that you didn't size the text boxes as we did on page 8 (see steps 19 and 20). You can correct this by returning to page 8 to decrease the height of the upper text box and increase the height of the lower text box.

**25.** Delete the end tag from the text box, and press the `Backspace` key to return the insertion point to the end of page 9. Then click the **Break Forward Link** button to end the continuation of the story.

The remaining two story continuations are in the correct order.

**26.** Use the skills you have learned to do the following:

- End the first story from page 2 (*How to convert a trial version*) in an evenly filled two-column text box on page 11.

- Continue the second story from page 2 (*Prepare, publish, and maintain*) into a two-column text box at the bottom of page 11, through pages 12, 13, and 14, to end on page 15.

> **Tip**  The text boxes on pages 12–15 are already linked, so you need only link the text boxes on pages 2, 11, and 12.

**27.** On the page sorter, right-click the **Page 16** button, click **Delete Page**, and then in the **Microsoft Office Publisher** message box, click **Yes** to confirm the deletion of the page, including the empty text box.

Page 16 now contains an empty two-column text box and a sidebar.

**28.** Drag the sidebar into the gray scratch area to the side of the page.

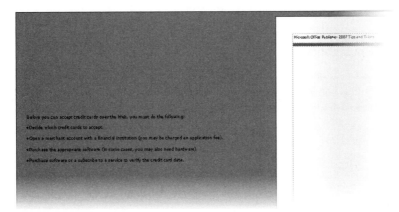

**See Also** For more information about the scratch area, see "Aligning and Stacking Objects" in Chapter 4, "Marketing Your Product, Service, or Organization."

29. Delete page 16, and then display page 15. Drag the sidebar from the scratch area to the empty space in the lower-left part of the page, and then size it to fit the column width and display its contents.

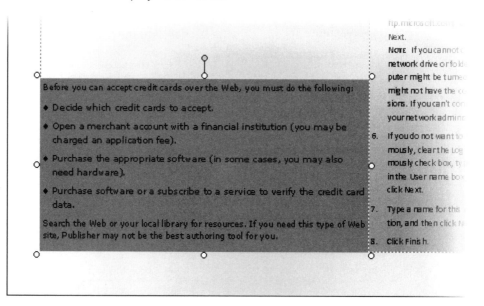

30. Display the publication in **Two-Page Spread** view, and change the **Zoom** level to **Whole Page**. Review the 16-page publication to see the results of your work.

> **Tip** Because this publication is double-sided, you must end with an even number of pages.

31. When you finish, update the page numbers in the table of contents on page 1 of the publication to reflect the final result.

**CLOSE** the publication without saving your changes.

# Editing and Proofing Content

For convenience, we have gathered together information about techniques for ensuring the accuracy of your text in the last topic of this chapter. However, editing and proofing are processes that are on-going throughout the development of a publication. The language you choose to convey your message should be polished, targeted to your audience, and error-free.

## Editing Content in Word

If you are familiar with Microsoft Office Word, you might be more comfortable crafting text by using Word tools and techniques than within a publication. Provided you have Word installed on your computer, you can simply right-click any text in a publication, point to Change Text, and then click Edit Story In Microsoft Word. A Word document containing the formatted text of the story opens, and Publisher indicates with cross-hatching that the text box(es) containing the story are unavailable for editing.

This pattern indicates that the story is open for editing in Word.

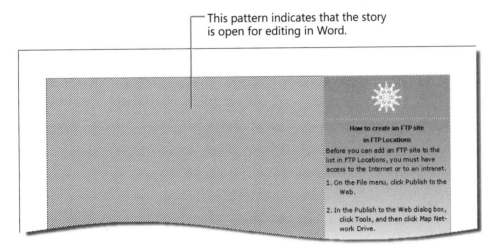

You can make content and formatting changes within the Word document. All the usual Word functions, including spelling and grammar review and word count, are available. When you finish, you close the document to return to Publisher. There is no need to save the document. (In fact, you cannot actually save the document, only a copy of it.) Your changes are immediately visible in the publication.

> **Tip** You can insert comments and track changes in the document within the current Word session. However, when you close the document, all changes are accepted and comments removed before the content reappears in Publisher.

# Correcting Spelling Errors

Before publishing a document, it is important to confirm that it contains no spelling errors. In this electronic age, there are few excuses for the spelling errors that frequently occur in professionally printed materials. (This seems to be a particularly prevalent issue with restaurant menus!) Even in a short publication—but much more so in a long publication—err on the safe side, and use the tools that the 2007 Microsoft Office system places at your disposal.

Publisher provides two tools to help you with the chore of eliminating spelling errors: the AutoCorrect and Spelling features. It doesn't include the grammar-checking feature available in Microsoft Office Word and Microsoft Office Outlook. However, if you display a story in Word as discussed earlier in this topic, you can run the full Spelling And Grammar feature. This is another great benefit of the easy interaction between Publisher and Word.

Have you noticed that Publisher automatically corrects some misspellings (such as *teh* to *the*) when you type them? This is the work of the AutoCorrect feature. AutoCorrect fixes common spelling and typing errors so that you don't have to. AutoCorrect comes with a long list of frequently mistyped words and their correct spellings.

> **Tip**   To open the AutoCorrect dialog box, click AutoCorrect Options on the Tools menu.

If you frequently mistype a word that AutoCorrect doesn't change, such as a difficult last name, you can add it to the list in the AutoCorrect dialog box.

If you deliberately mistype a word and don't want to accept the AutoCorrect change, you can undo the change by clicking the Undo button on the Standard toolbar or by pointing to the corrected word, clicking the AutoCorrect Options button that appears, and then clicking Change Back.

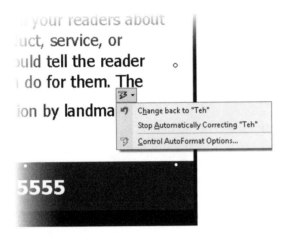

A great time-saving trick for longer publications is to use the AutoCorrect feature to avoid having to manually enter phrases that occur frequently in your publications. For example, if you work on a project in which you often have to type *For more information, see* followed by a topic or chapter reference, you can enter a short combination of letters that does not form a word, such as *fmi*, and the full phrase to the list in the AutoCorrect dialog box. Thereafter, when you type fmi and press the Spacebar, AutoCorrect replaces the letter combination with the full phrase.

Although AutoCorrect ensures that your documents are free of common misspellings, it cannot detect random typographical errors. To help you detect this type of error, Publisher includes the same spell-checking feature found in other Office programs. By default, Publisher checks your spelling as you type and indicates suspected spelling errors with red wavy underlines. You can correct an individual error by right-clicking it and selecting a suggested alternative, or you can check the spelling of a single story or the entire publication by clicking Spelling on the Tools menu and correcting errors in the Check Spelling dialog box.

Over-reliance on spelling checkers has led to a modern-day misspelling epidemic. People seem to believe that just because a publication has passed a spell-check, it must be OK, but there are numerous common mistakes in word usage, for example using "their" instead of "there," that will pass a spell-check. In critical publications, take the time to use the Word grammar checker, which will catch many of these. The grammar checker indicates questionable usage with a green wavy underline.

## Controlling Hyphenation

Many Publisher templates use text boxes to emulate the kinds of skinny-column layouts used in newspapers and magazines. To avoid leaving ugly gaps at the ends of lines and to make more content fit in less vertical space, Publisher automatically hyphenates multi-syllable words that fall within 0.25 inches of the edge of the text box.

For each story, you can change the width of the default hyphenation zone, or you can turn off this feature entirely by right-clicking the story you want to change, pointing to Proofing Tools, and then clicking Hyphenation to display the Hyphenation dialog box.

Clicking Manual displays a dialog box that moves from one hyphenated word to the next, allowing you to specify which words you want to hyphenate and how you want to hyphenate them.

> **Tip**  If you are going to manually hyphenate a story, ensure that all editing, including spell-checking, is complete before you begin. It is a waste of time to fine-tune hyphenation if later changes might rewrap lines and necessitate another round of adjustments.

To check the hyphenation settings of a story, you can click Options on the Tools menu, and then in the Options dialog box, click the Edit tab.

Changing the settings under Hyphenation on this tab affects only new text boxes, not existing ones.

In this exercise, you will create an advertisement, edit its content in Word, and check the spelling of the advertisement text. There is no practice file for this exercise.

> **BE SURE TO** start Publisher and close any open publications before beginning this exercise.

1. In the **Publication Types** list, click **Advertisements**.

   Publisher offers six monochromatic designs, each available in square and rectangular versions. If the active information set includes a logo, the design previews display the logo as well as the company name.

2. Under **Microsoft Office Online Templates**, click **View templates from Microsoft Office Online**.

If you have an active Internet connection, additional color advertisement templates provided by Microsoft (and possibly others) appear. Each Internet template is of a fixed size, and has a rating based on feedback from Office Online visitors.

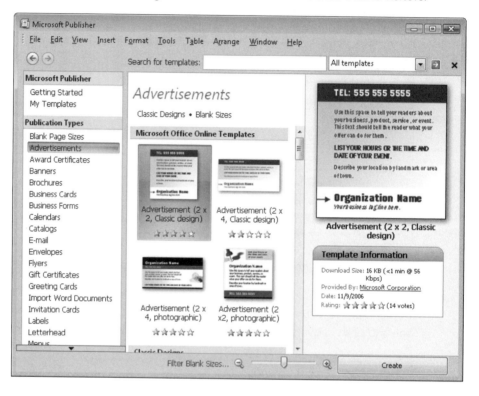

> **Troubleshooting**  If you don't have an active Internet connection, complete the exercise with any Publisher advertisement template.

3.  Select a template you like, and then click **Create**.

Publisher creates the selected advertisement. Placeholder text suggests the type of information you might include in each area of the advertisement. Blue dashes indicate placeholders linked to the information set.

4. Right-click the main placeholder text, point to **Change Text**, and then click **Edit Story in Microsoft Word**.

> **Troubleshooting** If Word is not installed on your computer, skip to step 5, and then follow along with the rest of this exercise in Publisher.

The text box becomes unavailable, and Word opens, displaying the placeholder text.

**See Also** For information about working in Word 2007, refer to our book *Microsoft Office Word 2007 Step by Step* (Microsoft Press, 2007).

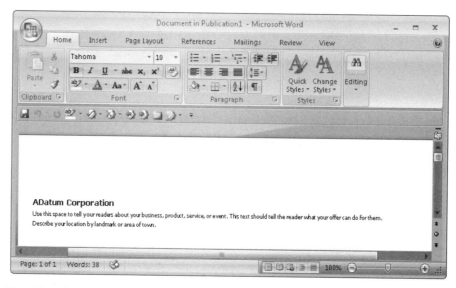

Your Word window might look different than the one shown here, depending on your settings.

5. In the text displayed in the document, remove a space from between two words to create a spelling error.

Word immediately indicates the error with a red wavy underline.

6. Close the document to return to Publisher. After a short pause, the changed text appears in the advertisement.

Publisher also indicates the misspelling with a red wavy underline.

> **Troubleshooting** If you don't see the wavy underline, point to Spelling on the Tools menu, and then click Spelling Options. Under When Correcting Spelling In Publisher, select the Check Spelling As You Type check box, and then click OK.

7. On the **Tools** menu, point to **Spelling**, and then click **Spelling**.

The Check Spelling dialog box opens, prompting you to correct the error. Your publication is visible behind the dialog box so that you can easily locate the indicated error in context—not important in a small publication such as this one, but very helpful in a longer publication.

You can accept the suggested correction or enter any replacement text you want in the Change To box. Then click Change to effect the replacement and move to the next detected error in the story (if there is one). After checking the story, Publisher offers to check the remainder of the publication.

8. Finish checking the spelling of the publication content, and then in the **Microsoft Office Publisher** dialog box that appears when the spelling check is complete, click **OK**.

> **CLOSE** the open publication without saving your changes, and if you are not continuing on to the next chapter, quit Publisher.

# Key Points

- You can create a publication of any length by using Publisher. To save time, plan the design, content, and layout of the publication in advance.

- When text does not fit exactly in a text box, you have many options, including resizing the text and the text box. You can have Publisher automatically resize text to fit the available space.

- You can insert, delete, and move pages in a publication. Each page retains its content. Moving pages that contain continued stories might result in story sections being out of order.

- You can edit story content in Word. All the program functionality other than saving the file is available.

- Publisher includes tools for checking and correcting spelling and for controlling hyphenation.

# Chapter at a Glance

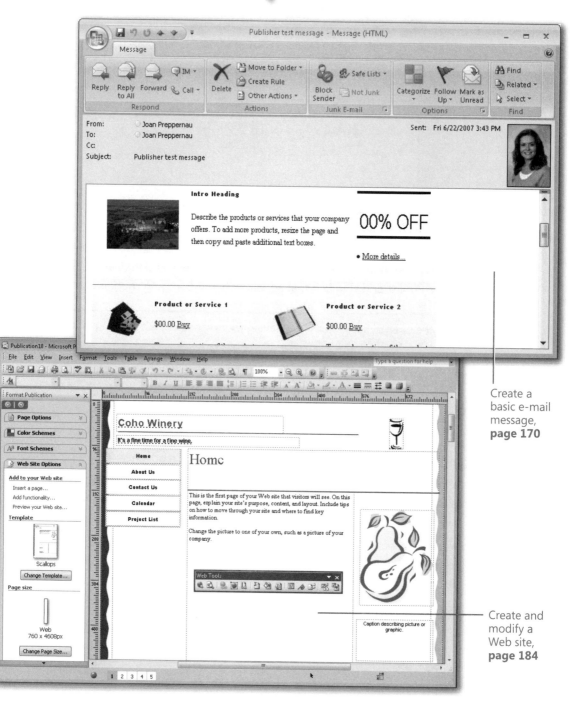

Create a basic e-mail message, **page 170**

Create and modify a Web site, **page 184**

# 6 Communicating Your Message Online

---

**In this chapter, you will learn to:**

✔ Create a basic e-mail message.

✔ Create a message from a multi-page publication.

✔ Create and modify a Web site.

---

Up to this point, we've worked with publications designed for print. But Microsoft Office Publisher 2007 does not limit you to printed publications—you can also create publications specifically designed to be sent as e-mail messages or published as Web sites. As with printed publications, Publisher provides a depth and breadth of design and layout choices that is truly impressive.

In this chapter, you will first create a simple one-page e-mail message publication, and then learn to send one or all pages of a multi-page publication by e-mail. Then you will create and modify a Web site.

**See Also** Do you need only a quick refresher on the topics in this chapter? See the Quick Reference entries on pages xxvii–xli.

> **Important** Before you can use the practice files in this chapter, you need to install them from the book's companion CD to their default location. See "Using the Book's CD" on page xvii for more information.

> **Troubleshooting** Graphics and operating system–related instructions in this book reflect the Windows Vista user interface. If your computer is running Windows XP and you experience trouble following the instructions as written, please refer to the "Information for Readers Running Windows XP" section at the beginning of this book.

# Creating a Basic E-Mail Message

E-mail has become a common, accepted, and for some people, preferred method of communicating with business associates and customers. You can use Publisher to easily create professional-looking HTML e-mail messages that incorporate and reinforce your brand.

**See Also** For more information about brand design elements, see "Building Your Brand" in Chapter 4, "Marketing Your Product, Service, or Organization."

With any one of these programs configured as your default e-mail application, you can create a message directly from Publisher so the publication content appears, fully formatted, in the message body:

- Microsoft Office Outlook (2003, 2007, or later)
- Outlook Express (version 5.0 or later), which is installed with Windows XP
- Windows Mail (version 6.0 or later), which is installed with Windows Vista

> **Tip** To set your default e-mail application, click Default Programs on the Start menu.

Message recipients do not need Publisher to view a publication that you send as a message; they can use any HTML-enabled e-mail application including Hotmail, AOL, or Yahoo Mail.

If you use an e-mail application other those listed above, you can send a publication with its design elements intact as an attachment to a message, in any of these formats:

- **Publisher.** You can send the Publisher (.pub) file. The recipient will need Publisher to view the publication, and will be able to make changes to it.

- **Portable Document Format (PDF).** After installing the free Save As PDF add-in from the Microsoft Download Web site, you can save a copy of a publication in PDF format. The recipient will need Adobe Acrobat or Adobe Reader (a free download from Adobe) to view the publication. PDF has become a common standard for secure distribution of all sorts of documents, because most people don't have the software necessary to make changes to PDF content.

- **XML Paper Specification (XPS).** After installing the free Save As XPS add-in from the Microsoft Download Web site, you can save a copy of a publication in XPS format. The recipient will need the XPS reader also (a free download from Microsoft) to view the publication. XPS is a relatively new document format, but it is rumored to have better support for gradients and transparencies, so might be preferable if your publication includes a lot of photographic elements.

> **Tip** You can create a PDF or XPS file by using the Save As command or the Publish As PDF Or XPS command; either produces the same result.

**See Also** For more information about saving in PDF or XPS format, see "Packaging Publications for Printing" in Chapter 3, "Creating Colorful Cards and Calendars."

- **Graphic image.** You can save a publication in several image file formats, including Portable Network Graphics Format (.png), Device Independent Bitmap (.bmp), Graphics Interchange Format (.gif), Tag Image File Format (.tiff), and JPEG File Interchange Format (.jpg). A publication saved in one of these formats is simply a large picture. This is the lowest common denominator and makes it more likely that any recipient can view your publication, regardless of what applications are installed on his or her computer. Choose the file type carefully, because some graphic file formats create very large files.

You can also save publications as text files, documents, and Web pages, but these formats will not necessarily preserve the design elements as you intend.

You can create an e-mail message from any of these three starting points:

- A design template
- A blank publication
- An existing publication of any format

    **See Also** For more information, see "Creating a Message from a Multi-Page Publication" later in this chapter.

Publisher 2007 includes design templates for these six types of e-mail messages:

- Invitations to an activity or presentation
- Product-marketing messages and catalogs
- Letter-style communications
- Newsletters

There are 44 designs available for each message type, for a total of 264 template choices, plus two blank templates. These templates are designed to provide a starting point for your message, but as with other publications, you can personalize the content as much or as little as you want.

> **Tip** A benefit of designing publications for online viewing is that you can use colors and photographic artwork without worrying about the cost of printing or the appearance of the printed version. Just remember to use graphics of a reasonable size and resolution to avoid clogging up the recipient's e-mail inbox with huge messages.

Two standard message page sizes are available: Short (5.818 x 11 inches) and Large (5.818 x 66 inches). The default design template content fills the 11 inch–high message format. Choose the page length most likely to accommodate your intended content. You can change the page size after you create the initial message. If you choose the longer page, you can reduce the page length to fit the final content—although you don't have to. When Publisher creates the e-mail message from the publication, it sizes the message to the precise length of the content.

> **Tip**  We asked a member of the Publisher development team why the message template width is set to 5.818 inches, but she didn't know why that odd measurement was chosen. It likely has to do with the width of an Outlook message window or Reading Pane. Do you know why? If so, we'd love to hear from you!

In this exercise, you will create an e-mail message from a template, format the message background, duplicate a group of objects, and send the message. There is no practice file for this exercise.

> **BE SURE TO**  install and configure Outlook, Outlook Express, or Windows Mail before beginning this exercise.

1. Start Publisher and display the **Getting Started** window. In the **Publication Types** list, click **E-mail**. Then scroll the center pane to see the available templates.

2. In the **Newer Designs** category, under **Product List**, click **PhotoScope**. In the **Customize** pane, set the **Color scheme** to **(default template colors)**, and the **Font scheme** to **(default template fonts)**. Then click **Create**.

   Publisher creates a one-page publication in the Large message format, containing placeholder design elements, graphics, and text for a catalog-like promotional message. If you have saved information in an information set, some details are filled in for you. (In this example, we're using information from a fictitious winery.)

3. Scroll the page to view the template content.

   After 11 inches (about two screens of information), the long page is blank.

   > **Tip**  To view the content without the distraction of the non-printing text box borders and margin indicators, click Boundaries And Guides on the View menu to turn off that feature.

> **Tip** The margins of the e-mail message templates are set to 0 inches.

Other Task Panes

**4.** In the **Format Publication** task pane, click the **Other Task Panes** button, and then click **Background**.

The Background task pane displays solid and patterned background options that coordinate with the current color scheme. Each of the five color choices is a 30% tint of one of the five Accent colors.

**5.** Click the pale gold (**30% tint of Accent 2**) color square, and then in the pattern list, click the **Gradient fill (horizontal)** icon (the third icon from the top of the left column, the one that is darker at the bottom than at the top).

Publisher changes the message background color to a gradient from white at the top of the message to gold at the bottom of the page. Because the page is so long, none of the background color is visible behind the message content. We'll discuss this later in the exercise.

**6.** Scroll the page to display the row containing **Product or Service 3** and **Product or Service 4**, and the horizontal line indicating the beginning of the row, at the top of the page.

Select Objects

7. On the **Objects** toolbar, click the **Select Objects** button. Point to the scratch area on the left side of the page, immediately above the horizontal line, and then drag a box to encompass the line and the two product listings that follow.

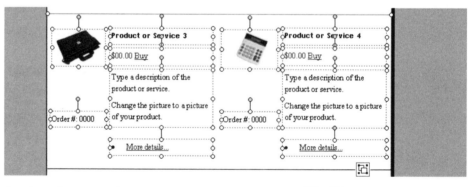

Drag to select multiple objects

8. Release the mouse button to select all the objects entirely within the selection box.

The Picture toolbar appears because one of the selected objects is a picture. Move the toolbar out of the way if necessary.

9. On the **Edit** menu, click **Copy**. (Or if you prefer, press Ctrl+C.)

10. Repeat step 7 to select all the objects in the area from the black horizontal line preceding the location details to the final text box.

11. Point to any one of the selected objects. When the insertion point changes to a four-headed arrow, drag the selected objects down the page to leave a blank section large enough for an additional row of catalog items.

12. Click in the blank area to release the selection, and then on the **Edit** menu, click **Paste**. (Or press Ctrl+V.)

A copy of the Product Or Services listing appears on top of the original.

13. Repeat step 11 to move the pasted objects into place below the originals. If necessary, adjust the location by pressing the ⬅, ➡, ⬆, and ⬇ keys.

    Your message now fills approximately 13.5 inches of the publication page, followed by more than 50 inches of blank page.

14. On the **File** menu, point to **Send E-mail**, and then click **E-mail Preview**.

    Publisher displays the HTML-format message in your default Web browser.

15. Right-click the HTML page, and then click **View Source**. (If you're using a browser other than Windows Internet Explorer, click the equivalent command.)

    A Notepad window opens, displaying the Web page source code. Nearly 20 pages of code are behind the reasonably simple e-mail message.

16. Scroll about one-third of the way through the document to display the code surrounding the actual content.

—The HTML code supporting the organization name

    Although the content in the message was not laid out in tables, Publisher has formatted the HTML content within tables to maintain the design.

17. Close the Notepad window and the Web page, and return to Publisher. Close the task pane if it is open.

**18.** On the **File** menu, point to **Send E-mail**, and then click **Send as Message**.

An e-mail message header and toolbar appear above the publication. The Accounts button appears on the toolbar only if you have multiple e-mail accounts configured within the default e-mail application.

E-mail message toolbar ⎯

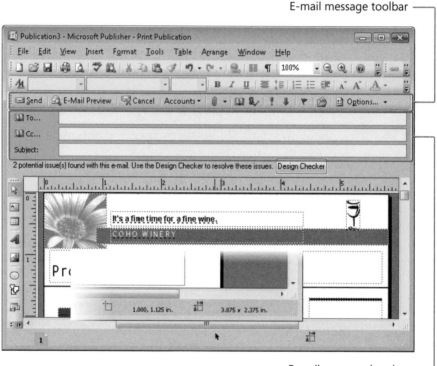

E-mail message header ⎯

The Design Checker automatically checks the publication for any elements that will change when converting the publication to a message. The Design Checker button appears below the message header only if the Design Checker identifies possible problems.

**19.** Click the **Design Checker** button.

The Design Checker task pane opens, displaying the results of its evaluation of the message. Because we haven't personalized the content of this message, we will not fix these issues before proceeding. You can find out which specific content is causing the errors by clicking an error message to go to the associated item.

20. In the message header, enter your own e-mail address in the **To** box, and Publisher test message in the **Subject** box. Then on the message toolbar, click the **Send** button.

21. Display your e-mail inbox and the received message.

Although the message publication page was set to 66 inches, the message itself ends just after the final text, and the gradient background is applied to within the length of the message.

**CLOSE** the message and the publication without saving your changes.

**E-Mail Merge**

You can send an e-mail message that you create in Publisher to a group of recipients stored in a data file—such as a database, workbook, delimited text file, or Outlook contacts list—by using the e-mail merge feature. You can select specific recipients from those in the data file and preview the message before sending it.

Follow these steps in an open publication:

1. On the **Tools** menu, point to **Mailings and Catalogs**, and click **E-mail Merge**.

   The E-mail Merge task pane displays the first of three steps you need to complete:

   - Creating or connecting to the recipient list
   - Preparing the publication
   - Sending the merged publication

2. Complete each step in the task pane, clicking the **Next** link as you finish each step.

You can select an account to send the message from and specify the message Subject text before sending the groups of messages.

By using the e-mail merge feature, it is nearly as easy to send 500 messages as it is to send only one. However, in order to avoid running afoul of anti-spam laws, we suggest you make sure you're up to date on the latest federal and state spam laws. For federal information, you can go straight to the source—the Federal Trade Commission—by visiting *www.ftc.gov/spam/*, or you can consult a more general-purpose Web site such as *www.spamlaws.com*. In general, federal regulations preclude you from sending misleading e-mail messages and require that you:

- Provide recipients a way to "opt out" of receiving any further messages from you (a request that you must honor within 10 business days).
- Provide clear identification of the e-mail message as an advertisement.
- Include your physical postal address.

# Creating a Message from a Multi-Page Publication

In this exercise, you will add pages to an e-mail message publication, send a single page of a multi-page publication, and send all pages of a multi-page publication.

**USE** the *WineTasting* and *BookSeries* publications. These practice files are located in the *Documents\Microsoft Press\SBS_Publisher2007\OnlinePublications* folder.

**BE SURE TO** install and configure Outlook, Outlook Express, or Windows Mail as your default e-mail application before beginning this exercise.

**OPEN** the *WineTasting* publication.

1. Close the **Format Publication** task pane, set the **Zoom** level to **100%**, and then review the content of this one-page e-mail publication promoting the first of a series of wine-education events.

   The boundaries and guidelines are turned off so that only the content is visible.

2. On the **Insert** menu, click **Page**. In the **Insert Page** dialog box, enter 3 in the **Number of new pages** box, and under **Options**, click **Duplicate all objects on page 1**. Then click **OK** to create three copies of the message page.

3. On page 2, change the date from *June 24th* to July 22nd, and on the following line, change *first* to second. On page 3, change the same information points to August 19th and third, and on page 4 to September 16th and fourth.

   The final date is longer than the others, causing the Text In Overflow indicator to appear.

4. Drag the left handle of the text box containing the date and time to the left until the text box is wide enough to accommodate its content.

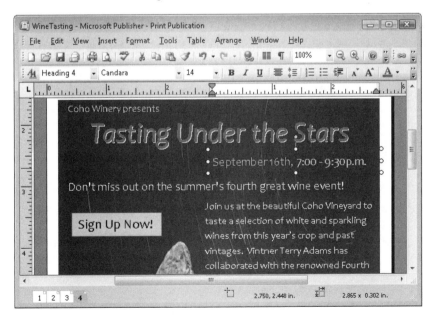

You now have one file containing separate e-mail messages promoting four separate events.

5. Display page 2—the message promoting the event on July 22nd.

6. On the **File** menu, point to **Send E-mail**, and then click **Send as Message**.

   The Send As Message dialog box opens.

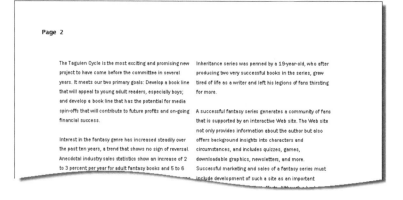

7. Click **Send current page only**, and then click **OK**.

   Publisher displays the e-mail message toolbar and message header, as well as a message from the Design Checker. If the task pane is displayed, it lists the 15 potential issues identified, including minor items such as non-Web-ready fonts.

8. On the **File** menu, point to **Send E-mail**, and then click **Cancel E-mail Message** to return to the publication editing interface.

Open

9. On the **Standard** toolbar, click the **Open** button. From the *Documents\Microsoft Press\SBS_Publisher2007\OnlinePublications* folder, open the *BookSeries* publication.

10. Close the **Format Publication** task pane, and then change the **Zoom** level to **100%**.

   This two-page publication consists of a cover page and a detailed book series overview.

11. Display page 2.

You need to send both pages of the publication embedded in an e-mail message.

**12.** On the **File** menu, point to **Send E-mail**, and then click **Send as Message**. In the **Send as Message** dialog box, click **Send all pages**, and then click **OK**.

The Send All Pages As Message dialog box opens.

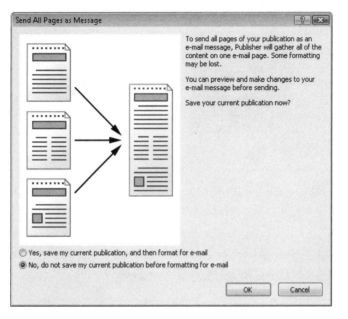

We haven't made changes to the publication, so there is no need to save it before creating the e-mail message.

**13.** With the **No** option selected, click **OK**.

Publisher creates an e-mail message containing the concatenated content of the document. Some graphic elements have changed.

The Format Publication task pane displays the Extra Content pane, listing design objects that Publisher couldn't automatically port to the e-mail message. These are not the same issues identified by the Design Checker.

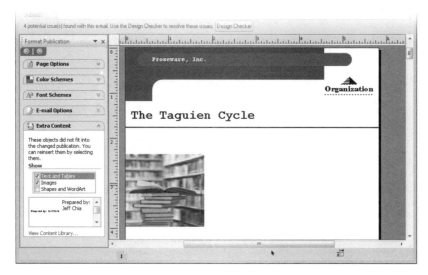

14. Scroll the list to view the three pieces of text Publisher couldn't identify locations for. Point to *Prepared by: Jeff Chia*, click the arrow that appears, and then click **Insert**.

A text box containing the selected text appears in the message. Move the text box to the right side of the page, under the horizontal line.

> **Tip** You can turn on boundaries and guides to view the text box outlines in the e-mail message.

15. Repeat step 14 to insert the proposal date under the author's name, and the document title at the beginning of the message. You might need to resize the text box containing *Series Proposal*.

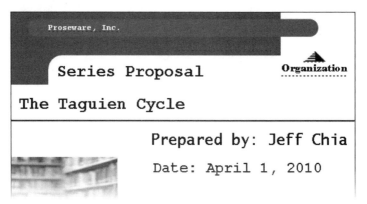

**16.** To the right of the first paragraph of the actual series description, delete the text box that contains the second instance of the document title. Then resize the text box containing the paragraph.

Notice that the text box still retains a link to the next text box.

The Taguien Cycle is the most exciting and promising new project to have come before the committee in several years. It meets our two primary goals: Develop a book line that will appeal to young adult readers, especially boys; and develop a book line that has the potential for media spin-offs that will contribute to future profits and on-going financial success.

Interest in the fantasy genre has increased steadily over the past ten years, a t that shows no sign of reversal. Anecdotal industry sales statistics show an increase of 2 to 3 percent per year for adult fantasy books and 5 to 6 percent for young adult fantasy books.  Each year Lucerne has published several fairytale/magic books for younger readers, but we do not currently offer anything sophisticated enough to appeal to

**17.** Enter your e-mail address in the **To** box and Publisher book proposal in the **Subject** box. Send the message, and then examine it when you receive it.

**CLOSE** the message and the publications without saving your changes.

## Publishing a Web Site

After you create a Web site, you can publish it to a Web server, a network server, an *FTP server*, or simply on your own computer. When you publish a site, Publisher saves the home page and one folder containing all the related pages, images, and sound files. The pages are saved as *filtered HTML files* that you can open by using any Web browser. Filtered HTML files upload faster

To ensure that a site functions as expected before you publish it to a Web server, publish it first to a folder on your local computer. Test the site and identify any necessary changes. Then return to the Web Site publication, make the changes, and republish the site. When you are satisfied with the site content, upload it to the Web server by using FTP or another utility provided by your ISP.

# Creating and Modifying a Web Site

Publisher doesn't immediately come to mind when thinking about Web site development applications, but it does actually provide a good basis for the development of a simple Web site. An advantage to using Publisher to develop your Web site or to develop Web pages is that you can very easily reinforce your brand by incorporating colors, fonts, and graphic elements from other publications. If you are a professional Web designer or want to create a site with a significant number of fancy programmatic elements, it is likely that you will use a more tailor-made Web site creation environment than Publisher.

Publisher 2007 includes 72 design templates (including No Design) and a blank template in three widths designed for varying screen resolutions (or if you want to purposefully limit the width of the site content). As with all publications, you can specify the font scheme and color scheme when you create it. You can also select the navigation bar location, choosing between a vertical bar on the left, a horizontal bar on the top, a horizontal bar on the bottom, and combinations thereof; or you can opt to go without a navigation bar.

As with printed publications, Publisher provides pre-designed Web pages that you can adapt to your needs. Most Web sites incorporate specific types of pages, and because the layout of each page type has become quite standardized, you can easily create the site you need based on the standard page templates. When you create a Web site, you can choose to start with a simple home page, or to start from a more complete base, you can select the Easy Web Wizard option when creating the site. When you choose this option, Publisher creates the home page and then displays the one-page Easy Web Site Builder, which asks a series of questions about the types of information you want to provide to site visitors, and adds pages to the initial site in response to your questions. If you have experience with Web site development you will probably find the Easy Web Site Builder unnecessary, but it provides a helpful starting point.

Publisher provides 30 Web page templates. These 9 common page types are available through the Easy Web Site Builder:

● **Home.** Every Web site has one home page—this is the page that appears when a visitor connects to your primary URL (for example, *www.microsoft.com*). To serve as the home page, the file name must be either *index* or *default*, because this is the name Web browsers look for. On the home page, you can welcome visitors, provide an overview of your organization (or the purpose of the site), and provide links, search engines, or other tools to help visitors find the information they are seeking.

● **About Us.** Use this page to tell people about your company or organization, your products or services, and your personnel.

- **Contact Us.** Use this page to tell people how to contact your company or organization and where you are located.

- **Product List With Links.** This consists of a one-page product list and six Product Detail pages. The default product list includes space for six products, each with specific areas for a picture, a description, an identifying code (such as the SKU or ISBN), the price, and a link to the associated Product Details page where you can provide additional pictures, a more detailed description, a feature list, and contact information.

- **Service List.** This page includes space for four services, each with specific areas for a picture, a description, an optional link to a Service Detail page (not created by default), and contact information.

- **Calendar.** This page displays a monthly calendar and a list of events, each with an optional link to an Event page (not created by default). Publisher creates a calendar for the current month; you can change the month by deleting the calendar object and replacing it with another from the Design Gallery.

- **Project List.** Although this is identified for use with projects, you can use the structure provided by this page to list a variety of information, including projects, clients, or activities. This page includes space for five entries, each with specific areas for a picture, a description, and an optional link to a Project Detail page (not created by default).

- **Employee List.** This page includes space for five entries, each with specific areas for a picture, a biography or job description, contact information, and an optional link to an Employee Detail page (not created by default).

- **Related Links.** From this page, you can provide visitors with links to other Web sites, or (less commonly) to specific pages of your site.

## Adding Pages to a Web Site

After you create a site, you can add blank or pre-designed pages to the site, and then personalize the content of those pages to fit your needs. Available page types include Calendar and Events, Employee (List and Detail), Frequently Asked Questions, Forms (Order, Response, and Sign-Up), General Information, Job List, Legal, News Articles, Photo (Gallery and Detail), Product (List and Detail), Project (List and Detail), Service (List and Detail), and Special Offer.

When you add a page to an existing site, you can choose whether to add it as a top-level page that appears on the site navigation bars, or simply to create the page and then manually link to it from another.

## Presenting Information in Tables and Lists

Some Publisher templates or template pages include placeholders for information that is formatted in a table or in a list. You can customize these placeholders with your own text the same way you would any other placeholder. You can also add a table or a list to any text box.

Information such as statistics or comparisons is best presented in a *table*. You can create two types of tables:

- A standard table is an object consisting of a series of cells laid out in columns and rows to form a grid. You can specify the width of the table and its columns, or have the column width adjust to fit its content. If necessary, you can merge or split cells to vary from the grid, but it is not as easy to make adjustments to a non-standard table. You can apply a variety of standard formats to a table to more clearly illustrate your content.

  The table object is independent of other objects, such as text boxes, so you can place, move, size, and format it independently of anything else on the page.

  | | Western | Central | Eastern |
  |---|---|---|---|
  | 1st Quarter | 4567.89 | 1234.56 | 3456.78 |
  | 2nd Quarter | 9876.54 | 6543.21 | 8765.43 |
  | 3rd Quarter | 1593.57 | 2671.68 | 4223.48 |
  | 4th Quarter | 4635.55 | 7559.45 | 8733.58 |
  | **Annual Total** | **$17631.57** | **$18008.90** | **$25179.27** |

- A *tabular list* is a series of paragraphs, each containing a specific number of pieces of information separated by tab characters. You set the tabs to align the information in columns. You can align the content of each column either by its left edge, its right edge, or its center point, and you can align a series of decimal numbers by the decimal point. You can format the space between columns as a line or a series of dots, dashes, or bullets.

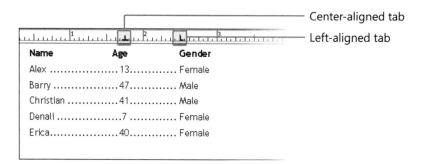

Center-aligned tab

Left-aligned tab

Information such as sequential steps or options is best presented in a *list*. You can create two types of lists:

● You present sequential information (such as step-by-step instructions) or a specified number of items (such as three choices) in a *numbered list*. A numbered list can have multiple levels, each with a specific alphanumeric numbering system and indent level.

> To get to the coffee shop, follow these directions:
>
> 1. Take I-15 North to Camino del Norte.
>
> 2. At the end of the exit, turn left.
>
> 3. Go through two intersections, and then turn left onto Dove Canyon.
>
> 4. Turn left at the first light.
>
> The coffee shop is in the northwest corner of the shopping center.

● You present non-sequential information or an unspecified number of items in a *bulleted list*. A bulleted list can also have multiple levels, each denoted by a specific bullet character and indent level.

> You can create many types of publications by using Publisher, including the following:
>
> • Brochures
> • Cards
>   ⇒ Business cards
>   ⇒ Greeting cards
>   ⇒ Postcards
> • Certificates
>   ⇒ Award certificates
>   ⇒ Gift certificates
> • Newsletters
> • Web sites

For either type of list, you enter each list item in its own paragraph, apply the list format, and if necessary set the level; Publisher inserts the numbers, letters, or roman numerals indicating the series order.

## Adding Existing Publications to a Web Site

You can add another publication to a Web site; for example, you can add a menu to a restaurant site or a resume to a personal site. To add a publication as a top-level page to a Web site, follow these steps:

1. Open the publication in Publisher. On the **File** menu, click **Publish to the Web**.

2. In the **Publish to the Web** dialog box, browse to your Web site directory structure, name the file, and then click **Save** to save an HTML version of the file.

3. Open the site in Publisher. Click anywhere on the navigation bar, and then click the **Navigation Bar Options** button that appears.

Navigation Bar
Options

**Navigation Bar Properties**

Name:

Main Navigation Bar

Links:

Home
About Us
Contact Us
Product List
Service List
Calendar
Project List
Employee List
Related Links
Event

Add Link...

Remove Link

Modify Link...

Move Up

Move Down

☑ Update this navigation bar with links to new pages that are added to this publication.

OK     Cancel     Help

4. In the **Navigation Bar Properties** dialog box that opens, click **Add Link**.

5. In the **Add Link** dialog box, in the **Link to** list, click **Existing File or Web Page**. Then in the **Look in** pane, browse to the HTML version of the file.

6. In the **Text to display** box, enter the text you want to appear on the navigation link. Then click **OK**.

   In the Navigation Bar Properties dialog box, the linked file appears in the Links list.

7. To change the position of the linked file on the navigation bar, click the **Move Up** and **Move Down** buttons. When the navigation links appear in the order you want, click **OK** in the **Navigation Bar Properties** dialog box.

## Adding Text and Graphics to a Web Page

You customize the placeholder content of a Web site in the same way you would the content of any other publication you work with in Publisher. You can replace or remove placeholder text and graphics; add, remove, or rearrange text boxes and images; and link text boxes to control the flow of content. Publisher makes it simple for you to do all these things regardless of your experience with Web programming languages.

## Adding Features to a Web Page

You can format many of the same page features for a Web page as you can for a printed publication page, including *bookmarks*, hyperlinks between locations, and a background color, pattern, or picture. Although Publisher does not provide as many bells and whistles as Microsoft Office FrontPage, Microsoft Office SharePoint Designer, Microsoft Expression Web, or similar programs intended solely for Web design, it does make it easy to insert background sounds, form controls, and *hot spots*, and to attach *metadata* to a page to help search engines locate it. You can implement other functionality, such as a hit counter, by inserting the necessary HTML code on the page (by using the Insert HTML Fragments command).

In this exercise, you will create a Web site based on a template, add and configure a form, customize the navigation bar, and preview the site. There is no practice file for this exercise.

> **BE SURE TO** start Publisher and close any open publications before beginning this exercise.

1. In the **Publication Types** list, click **Web Sites**. Scroll the page to see the available templates. Then in the **Classic Designs** category, click **Scallops**.

2. Under **Customize** in the right pane, set the **Color scheme** to **(default template colors)** and the **Font scheme** to **(default template fonts)**.

3. Under **Options**, set the **Navigation bar** to **Vertical only**. Select the **Use Easy Web Wizard** check box, and then click **Create**.

   Publisher creates the home page of a Web site based on the selected template, and the Easy Web Site Builder dialog box (shown earlier in this chapter) opens.

   > **Tip** In a Web Site publication, the ruler helpfully displays measurements in pixels.

4. In the **Easy Web Site Builder** dialog box, select the following check boxes:
   - Tell customers about my business
   - Tell customers how to contact us
   - Display a calendar or schedule
   - Display a list of projects or activities

As you select each check box, the page or pages Publisher will create for that purpose appear on the right side of the dialog box.

**5.** Select any other pages that interest you, and then click **OK**.

Publisher creates the page or pages to support each selection. The Web Tools toolbar appears.

Content from the Business Information Set

Task pane scroll bar — Navigation bar — Page title

**6.** On the navigation bar, note the order of the Web site page links. Then on the page sorter, click each page in turn.

The navigation bar reflects the order of the pages within the publication. It is customary for the Contact Us page to be the last entry on the navigation bar.

**7.** On the page sorter, drag page 3 (Contact Us) to the end of the publication.

The navigation bar does not change to reflect the new page order. We'll return to this issue later in the exercise.

**8.** Display page 4, the Project List. Then in the **Web Site Options** pane, click **Insert a page**.

The Insert Web Page dialog box opens, displaying a list of all the available page types.

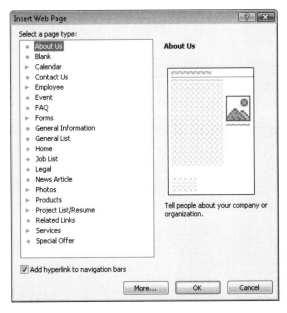

**9.** In the **Select a page type** list, click **Forms**, and then click **Sign-up Form**. With the **Add hyperlink to navigation bars** check box selected, click **OK** to create the page.

Publisher creates the form as page 5, but inserts the corresponding page link at the end of the navigation bar, labeled simply *Form*.

Navigation Bar Options

**10.** Click anywhere on the navigation bar, and then click the **Navigation Bar Options** button that appears.

The Navigation Bar Properties dialog box opens.

**11.** In the **Links** list, click **Contact Us**. Click **Move Down** three times to place the page link in the same order that the pages appear on the page sorter.

**12.** In the **Links** list, click **Form**, and then click **Modify Link**.

**13.** In the **Modify Link** dialog box, replace *Form* in the **Text to display** box with Register Now! Then click **Change Title**.

The Enter Text dialog box opens.

**14.** In the **Enter Text** dialog box, replace *Form* in the **Page title** box with Register Now! Then click **OK** in each of the three open dialog boxes.

The form created by Publisher is a fully functional information submission form. Before you can publish the site, you must specify the action to occur when a site visitor submits the form.

**15.** Scroll to the bottom of the form, right-click the **Submit** button, and then click **Format Form Properties**.

The Command Button Properties dialog box opens.

**16.** Clear the **Button text is same as button type** check box, and in the **Button text** box, replace *Submit* with Register. Then click **Form Properties**.

> **Tip** Within Publisher, you can move between site pages either by clicking page numbers on the page sorter, or by pressing Ctrl and then clicking the page link in the navigation bar.

The Form Properties dialog box opens.

**17.** Under **Data retrieval method**, click **Send data to me in e-mail**. Under **Data retrieval information**, enter your e-mail address in the **Send data to this e-mail address** box that appears, and enter Publisher Form Test in the **Subject of e-mail** box. Then click **OK** in each of the two open dialog boxes.

**18.** On the form page, click the **Register** button once to select it, and then press the ← key several times to align the left edges of the button and the **Exp. date** box.

**19.** In the **Web Site Options** pane, click **Preview Web site**.

The site opens in your default browser.

**20.** Click the navigation pane buttons to move between pages and see the types of content created by the page templates.

Because the site has not yet been published, submitting the form will result in an error.

> **CLOSE** the Web site and the publication without saving your changes.

# Key Points

- If you use recent versions of Outlook, Outlook Express, or Windows Mail, you can generate an e-mail message form containing the formatted content of a single-page or multi-page publication directly from Publisher.

- You can save a publication in several formats appropriate for sending as an attachment to an e-mail message.

- You can create a fully featured Web site with a wide variety of pre-designed pages, and edit the site content just as you would any other publication.

# Glossary

**alleys** The spaces between the system of columns and rows comprising a grid.

**back matter** Portions of a publication that are typically located after the main content, such as an index, glossary, or bibliography.

**background** The design, such as color, texture, or picture, that appears behind your text or other publication objects.

**baseline guides** Horizontal lines used to help align text or design elements.

**bleed** The extent to which an element extends beyond the edge of the printed page.

**bleed marks** Horizontal and vertical lines indicating the bleed on a printed page. See also *crop marks*.

**bookmark** A location or selection of text in a file that you name so that you can later refer or link to it.

**brand elements** The name, logo, fonts, colors, and design in materials sent to customers that identify a company or organization.

**bulk mail** A large amount of mail (at least 500 pieces), which the post office discounts to a bulk rate from the regular cost of postage.

**bulleted list** A method of listing an unordered series or unspecified number of concepts, items, or options.

**card stock** A heavier weight of paper, also known as postcard paper.

**character formatting** Formatting such as font, size, style, effect, color, or spacing that you can apply to selected text characters to vary the appearance.

**character spacing** The distance between characters in a line of text, which can be adjusted by using tracking, kerning, and scaling.

**chevron** The « or » characters that surround data fields in the publication.

**clip art** License-free graphics that often take the form of cartoons, sketches, or symbolic images, but can also include photographs, audio and video clips, and more sophisticated artwork.

**CMYK** A method of creating colors by using combinations of cyan, magenta, yellow, and black. See also *process colors*.

**color gradient** A visual effect in which a color gradually changes from light to dark, from dark to light, or from one color to another.

**color scheme** The set of default colors specified for a template or publication.

**compress** To shrink the file size of an image, document, or other file.

**connection point** The end point of a line that connects two shapes. Moving a connected shape also moves the line, maintaining the relationship between the connected shapes.

**continuing a story** The process of connecting text boxes so that text that doesn't fit in one text box flows into another text box.

**coordinates** The location of the insertion point or of the upper-left corner of an element, expressed as the distance from the upper-left corner of the page.

**copyfit** To format text so that it fits within a text box.

**copyright** A form of protection for artistic or literary works.

**crop** To hide or cut away the vertical or horizontal edges of a graphic that you don't want to show.

**crop marks** Horizontal and vertical lines indicating the four corners of a publication page, when printing a publication on a sheet of paper that is larger than the desired output.

**data fields** Categories of information that correspond to fields (usually columns) in a data source.

**data source** A file that contains the information to be merged into a publication.

**desktop publishing** The use of a specialized computer program to create professional-quality documents that combine text and other visual elements in non-linear arrangements.

**direct mail** A service provided by some copy and print shops, in which they merge your publication and data source while printing, sort the printed pieces, and then deliver them to the post office, ready for bulk mailing.

**duplex** The capability of a printer to print on both sides of the paper.

**File Transfer Protocol (FTP) server** A server that can be used to upload or download files to the Internet.

**filtered HTML files** HTML files, created from an Office document or publication, that contain no Office-specific codes. Filtered HTML files are smaller than unfiltered files and require less bandwidth to upload.

**font** The style set you specify for your text, consisting of alphabetic characters, numbers, and symbols that share a common design.

**font color** The specific color of the text, chosen from a palette of harmonious colors or custom colors you specify.

**font effect** The enhancement of a font, such as underlining, small capital letters (small caps), or shadows.

**font size** The measurement of the font in points. See *points*.

**font style** Character formatting such as regular (or plain), italic, bold, and bold italic.

**footprint** The amount of space required by an element.

**frame** The outline around a text box or other object. You can move an object by dragging its frame.

**front matter** Portions of a publication that are typically located before the main content, such as a table of contents or an introduction.

**gallery** A grouping of thumbnails that display options visually.

**grayscale** Shades of gray in a graphic.

**grid** A system of columns and rows that imposes a logical layout on the content of the publication and provides visual continuity from one page to the next.

**grid guides** The horizontal and vertical lines that make up a grid.

**grid units** The division of space within a publication. The default number of units is determined by the purpose of the publication and the number and type of elements to be included in the layout.

**group** To associate multiple shapes or objects so they are treated as one object. See also *regroup* and *ungroup*.

**handles** The points surrounding a text box or other object that you can move to change the size or shape of the box.

**hot spot**  A hyperlink that is not anchored to specific text or to a bookmark.

**hover**  To pause the pointer over an object, such as a menu name or button, for a second or two to display more information, such as a submenu or ScreenTip. See also *ScreenTip*.

**HSL**  A method of identifying a color in terms of its position in the rainbow (hue), its purity or vividness (saturation), and its brightness (luminance).

**information set**  A customized group of information, about either an individual or an organization, that can be used to quickly fill in appropriate places in publications, such as business cards and flyers.

**keyword**  A word associated with a Publisher template. You can type a keyword in the Search For Templates box at the top of the Getting Started window and then click the Search button to display thumbnails of the templates.

**layout**  The designation of where objects are placed in the publication.

**leaf**  The front and back of one page of a publication.

**line break**  A manual break that forces the text that follows it to the next line. Also called a *text wrapping break*.

**list**  A way to present sequential (numbered) or non-sequential (bulleted) information. See also *bulleted list* and *numbered list*.

**logo**  A graphic or text or a combination of the two that identifies a company or organization—or its products or services—in a unique way. It is used in addition to or instead of the name in printed and online materials and is part of the effort to present those materials in a consistent way that promotes brand recognition.

**mail merge**  A process that combines the static information in a publication with the variable information in a data source (a mailing list or any other type of database) to create one copy of the merged publication for every record in the data source.

**margin guides**  A guide on the top, bottom, left, and right sides of a page that are used to define its margins. Most contents of a page are within the margin guides.

**master page**  The page in which the overall publication design is controlled. Anything that appears on the master page appears on every page. Most master page elements can be changed only on the master page.

**metadata**  Information inserted in a Web publication that helps search engines locate it.

**Microsoft Clip Organizer**  A tool in which you can arrange clip art images, pictures, audio clips, and video clips stored in different locations.

**Microsoft Office Online**  A Web site from which you can download publication templates.

**newsletter**  A periodic publication containing information of interest to a specific group—for example, employees of a company or members of a club or other organization.

**numbered list**  A method of listing sequential information or a specified number of items.

**object**  A finite element, such as a graphic or a text box, that can be moved, sized, stacked, grouped, and formatted in various ways.

**page layout**  The arrangement of elements in the publication.

**page sorter**  One or more page-shaped controls, located in the lower-left corner of the Publisher window, that represent each page of the publication and can be used to go to, rearrange, or work with publication pages.

**Pantone Matching System (PMS)** A proprietary system developed by Pantone, Inc. to give designers in color-critical industries such as publishing, packaging, decorating, and architecture the means to communicate with printers and manufacturers.

**paragraph formatting** The settings you use to change the look of a paragraph.

**paragraphs** Created by typing text and pressing the Enter key. A paragraph can be a single word, a single sentence, or multiple sentences.

**patent** A form of protection for inventions.

**picture** An illustration or scanned photograph.

**placeholder** Boxes inserted into the publication, in which you can enter text or pictures.

**points** A measurement unit of approximately 1/72 of an inch. Font sizes expressed in points are measured from the top of the character ascenders to the bottom of the character descenders.

**Portable Document Format (PDF)** A device-independent and resolution-independent file format for representing documents containing any combination of text and images.

**process colors** A method of printing colors by using four inks (cyan, magenta, yellow, and black) to produce all other colors. See also *CMYK*.

**public domain** Belonging to the public, such as text or artwork that anyone can use in a publication.

**publication** A file created for distribution, such as to advertise for promotional events or to send birthday wishes.

**publication type** The style of a publication, such as a flyer, a business card, or a greeting card.

**read-only** A setting applied to a publication to protect it from inadvertent changes.

**recto** In a two-page spread, the right, odd-numbered page of the spread.

**regroup** After ungrouping a group of shapes, to make them one object again. See also *group* and *ungroup*.

**RGB** A method of identifying a color in terms of a combination of red, green, and blue.

**rotate** To change the angle of a graphic or text box.

**rotating handle** A green handle, available when a text box is active, that you can drag to change the angle of the text box and the text within it.

**ruler guides** A non-printing horizontal or vertical guide that you can align with any point on the ruler.

**saddle-stitching** A type of binding in which pages are stapled in the middle and then folded to create a booklet. Also called *stapling*.

**scratch area** The gray area around the page in Publisher in which you can place objects for later use.

**ScreenTip** A small window that appears when you point to a program element, usually containing explanatory information.

**section opener** A special page that signifies the starting point of a new section of a publication.

**sections** Topics in a publication that fall logically into groups, such as parts, subjects, or time periods.

**service mark** A registration of your company's name or logo, used to identify the source of a service.

**signature** A printed sheet that will be folded into a specific number of pages (often 16). Pages are arranged on the sheet to be in the proper sequence and orientation after the sheet is folded.

**silk-screening** A printing technique that creates a sharp-edged image by using a stencil.

**snap** To automatically align an object with the nearest ruler mark, guide, or other object.

**spot colors** A method of specifying and printing colors in which each color is printed with its own ink. See also *process colors*.

**spread** Represents the facing left and right pages of a publication.

**stacked** A term used to describe objects overlapping each other. The default stacking order is determined by the order in which objects are inserted, with the first object at the bottom of the stack and the last object at the top.

**stapling** A type of binding in which pages are stapled in the middle and then folded to create a booklet. Also called *saddle-stitching*.

**status bar** An area across the bottom of the program window that gives information about the current document.

**story** Any discrete block of text that occupies a text box or a set of linked text boxes. It can be a single paragraph or multiple paragraphs.

**style** A collection of character and paragraph formatting.

**table** Information presented in a grid that consists of a series of cells laid out in columns and rows.

**tabular list** A series of paragraphs, each containing a specific number of pieces of information separated by tab characters.

**template** A basic publication containing elements that you can modify.

**text box** An object that can be sized to fit the text it contains. You can type text directly into the text box, paste text from another file, or insert the entire contents of another file.

**texture** A pattern or gradient applied to the background of a publication to make it appear more three dimensional.

**thumbnail** A small graphic representing choices available in a gallery or pages in a document.

**title bar** An area at the top of the program window that displays the name of the active document.

**trademark** A registration of your company's name or logo, used to identify the source of a product.

**ungroup** To separate a group of objects into individual objects. See also *group* and *regroup*.

**verso** In a two-page spread, the left, even-numbered page of the spread.

**washout** An effect applied to a graphic or text that results in muted shades of the original color.

**watermark** A word or image that appears faintly in the background of a publication or other document.

**word processing** The use of a computer or typewriter to create text documents.

**WordArt** Text objects you can create with ready-made effects to which you can apply additional formatting options. Used to visually enhance the text in headings or other short phrases.

# Index

# D

# E

# What do you think of this book?

# We want to hear from you!

Do you have a few minutes to participate in a brief online survey?

Microsoft is interested in hearing your feedback so we can continually improve our books and learning resources for you.

To participate in our survey, please visit:

**www.microsoft.com/learning/booksurvey/**

...and enter this book's ISBN-10 number (appears above barcode on back cover*).
As a thank-you to survey participants in the United States and Canada, each month we'll randomly select five respondents to win one of five $100 gift certificates from a leading online merchant. At the conclusion of the survey, you can enter the drawing by providing your e-mail address, which will be used for prize notification only.

Thanks in advance for your input. Your opinion counts!

\* Where to find the ISBN-10 on back cover

ISBN-13: 000-0-0000-0000-0
ISBN-10: 0-0000-0000-0

Example only. Each book has unique ISBN.

No purchase necessary. Void where prohibited. Open only to residents of the 50 United States (includes District of Columbia) and Canada (void in Quebec). For official rules and entry dates see:

**www.microsoft.com/learning/booksurvey/**